Peace Rites

Carla DeSola

Thomas Kane, Editor

THE PASTORAL PRESS
Washington, DC

Photo Credits:
>   Mev Puleo, pages 15, 29, 55
>   Beverly Hall, pages 5, 43, 69
>   Randy Monceaux, back cover

ISBN: 1-56929-006-7

The Pastoral Press
225 Sheridan Street, N.W.
Washington, D.C. 20011
(202) 723-1254

The Pastoral Press is the publications division of the National
Association of Pastoral Musicians, a membership organization of
musicians and clergy dedicated to fostering the art of musical
liturgy.

Printed in the United States of America

With thanks
to
Teresina and Joseph Havens,
wise and wonderful guides;
Arthur Eaton,
sustainer, collaborator, husband;
Tomaso,
colleague, friend and editor;
Allan Tung, Omega PeaceArts
and the
Cathedral of St. John the Divine;
dancers, students, peacemakers.

Contents

Foreword

George Orwell wrote that "Fishing is the opposite of war." Ever since reading that I have wanted to say, "George, ask the fish."

Especially now, at the end of this tragic century, human beings are trying to imagine a new way to live with each other, a common life beyond war. As the threat of nuclear holocaust recedes and economic forces more and more dominate the interplay of nations, the question is desperately put: will the world conflict that for so long has been fueled by fear draw new energy from simple greed? As human beings in the northern hemisphere restructure economies around the goal of increased consumption, their brothers and sisters in the south are confronted with new levels of social collapse that make the relevant goal not consumption but survival. During the cold war the poor peoples of Africa, Latin America and Asia were pawns in the great East-West power game. Now that the game has become more economic than military, those peoples have been swept off the board. They are not "players" in the global economy. They are not at the table. They are not visible. They do not exist.

George, ask the people.

They *do* exist. Every human person alive on this planet is a son or daughter of God. Every one has rights to food and sustenance, to love and respect, to wonder and joy. One person's right to "consume" does not pre-empt an entire family's right to survive. The world needs a new peace movement—one that *sees* and *celebrates* and defends every person in the way that the creating and sustaining God does. As this bloody century draws to a close, the work of peacemakers has never been more important, and perhaps never more difficult. Yet peacemaking will thrive if it draws its energy from a deeply felt and disciplined experience of spiritual oneness—our oneness with each other and with the God whom we have in common as the creator and sustainer.

And that is why this workbook is a blow for peace. At a remote retreat center in the hills of Massachusetts many years ago—the war in Vietnam was still raging—I first encountered Carla DeSola's special gift. We were a group of disenchanted, perhaps overly intellectual, slightly inhibited activists and students when Carla invited us to dance. Carla DeSola is not only an exquisitely beautiful dancer, a gifted artist, but also a master teacher. With her help, we reclaimed that enabling sense of oneness—oneness within ourselves as body, mind, soul and heart move together; oneness with each other as diverse individual rhythms synchronize; oneness with the people far away, waging and suffering the violence. This workbook is the distillation of Carla DeSola's long experience as a dancer and master teacher, an embodiment of her key insight—that *dancing* is the opposite of war.

Ask the dancers. They will confirm it.

That is what, for many years, Thomas Kane has been doing. Another artist who is also a priest and a theologian, Father Kane is himself a long-committed worker for peace and justice. I know him as a friend. I remember standing with him in deep silence two decades ago in what the Spanish call the Valley of the Dead, a memorial to the million who died in the Civil War, the conflict that gave us mass killing. Tom Kane is large-hearted enough to enter fully into such tragedy, yet without losing the rare, infectious sparkle of wit and joy that mark him as a man. Joy marks every page of this workbook. Father Kane has traveled the world as an apostle of oneness, studying the rituals of various peoples with a particular eye on the religious use of dance. No one understands dance as a universal language, and as worship, better than he does. Carla DeSola could not have found a better and more congenial collaborator.

What these two gifted believers have done we can all do now—put our experience and our skill, our hearts, souls, minds and bodies at the service of a new image of what it means to be a human being on this planet; a son or daughter of God in a new century. Peace requires us to reinvent not only our economies but ourselves. But to do that we must rediscover the basic human wishes, impulses and gifts that make us one. And a way to do that, these masters suggest, is to fall silent, to be still, to let the music come, the holiness, to let it move us, alone and together.

Shall we dance?

James Carroll

- James Carroll is the author of many novels, most recently **Memorial Bridge**, *about a general and his son, a war resister.*

Introduction

We wish there were one rite of peace that we could dance
. . . a peace rite that would flow from our heart and limbs to the
world and put an end to war. Yet we haven't found it, so we train
our hearts, bend our backs a bit, learn to dance along the path with
peace-guided instincts. It would be great to dance for peace in an
earthshaking way. But, perhaps, one simple gesture may do just as
well . . . like a small flower within the reach of a child.

From what sources come our persistent, personal desire
for peacemaking and belief that it matters? Why does the possibil-
ity of being pulled apart by some destructive or malevolent force
seem so terrifying? We are aware of the potential volcanos within
and we don't want to be overwhelmed. Dancing is our way to
withstand and counteract those forces. This means searching
within, listening to the words of Jesus, responding to the stirrings
of the Spirit, and expressing this meaning through dance.

So much has happened since we began putting these
exercises together. The cycles of violence seem to continue
endlessly, and are distressingly similar. We wonder when will we
learn the way to peace. And so, we continue our search. It seems
beautiful to place our faith in the God who led Job to ponder such
mysteries as the Pleides, asking him to trust in God's purpose. It
strengthens us to believe Jesus when he says, ". . . be of good
cheer, I have overcome the world" (Jn 16:33).

With the Spirit, we pray these exercises and rites will
bring healing to some, and make a contribution to the way of
peace.

-Carla DeSola and Thomas A. Kane, C.S.P.

About PeaceRites

PeaceRites is a series of movement workshops about the creating of peace. The focus of these explorations is ourselves. The materials are our very bodies and souls, interacting with others and our environment. The workshops have been designed by reflecting on Scripture and prayer and shaped through the medium of dance.

The objectives of *PeaceRites* are to reinforce those already committed to working for peace, and to challenge others to explore the meaning of peace through shared communal experiences. Participants need no formal dance training. The work is of value to both dancers and non-dancers. Through sound, movement, and imagery, peacemaking becomes more dynamic, taking on a reality and urgency that go beyond words.

PeaceRites accomplishes its objectives by

- developing personal awareness of peacemaking through dance, music, and the spoken word;
- demonstrating ways to be responsive and open with one another, by removing inner barriers to closeness, learning to yield into the goodness of peace;
- portraying in a vivid way the effects of isolation and apathy on both individuals and society; and
- providing opportunities for full sensory and physical involvement, by affirming and liberating the spirit.

PeaceRites is divided into five components. As workshops, they are: (1) Disarming the Self; (2) In Touch With Others; (3) Dancing on Holy Ground; and (4) The Way of the Beatitudes. It concludes with The Peace Rite, a joyful and solemn ritual celebration. Each workshop is designed as a complete unit, comprised of the following:

1

- Introduction to the theme
- Invocation (prayer of centering)
- Warm-Up (general loosening-up exercises)
- Theme Work (movement specific to the theme)
- Study (searching into the heart of the theme; combining dance, Scripture, music, and meditation; members work alone and in groups)
- Rite (a concluding ceremony centered on the theme to unify and strengthen the participants)
- Workshop Material

Why Dance?

"In God we live, and move, and have our being." Dance celebrates all movement. It is based on the beat of our heart, the inhalation and exhalation of breath, and the passion of our feelings. It includes the stillness of pure contemplation. Dance is close to the primal sources of all spirituality.

We move, and through movement learn from our senses, taking in, with eyes, ears and feelings the wonders as well as the horrors of the world. Dance is a way of practicing feeling our responses. We have to practice feeling because too often we are taught to avoid feeling pain, and therefore accept violence, and then accept war. And we are also taught to avoid feelings of joy, and therefore live within walls that separate us from our deepest selves. In the process of integrating feelings, thoughts, and perceptions through physical expression and inner prayers, body and spirit can be transformed. Feelings that seemed heavy, forces that seemed irreconcilable can both become lighter and more fluid. Dance arouses and opens the way to life-giving actions which conquer deadly inertia. Movement grounds us in the roots of our own experience of God, and of life. We can know, from the inside, how beauty feels and evolves. Dance can lead us by its own gifts, to "knowing the things that make for peace."

Dance, expressing our spirituality, can become a healing, connecting, and liberating force in our lives. Dance heals. Through focussed movement prayers, we become more attuned with our intuitive self. From this experience arise new feelings, strengths and movements. In this dynamic milieu dance helps to release personal blocks and awaken unexplored energies within us. These dance-transformative experiences also subtly change human interrelationships.

Dance connects us. It bridges differences in mind, body, and spirit. As an antidote to alienation, dance is a unifying experience, linking us to others. We feel our personal and spiritual boundaries expand as we connect to the ever larger awareness of the presence of God, in the space around us and on the ground where we move. Dance frees. It invites us to let go of our pre-conditioned self images and experience the freedom of a child. In dance, new movement patterns emerge as we intermingle, in touch with the energies and gifts of each other.

Dance opens and connects us with the on-going, evolving beauty and power of creation. Dance is independent of race, creed, and color. As a form of folk art, it has always served to unite a culture. In our day, dance is available to all, helping us to appreciate the richness and variety of diverse cultures and spiritualities.

Notes for Workshop Leaders

The role of the workshop leader is as important to the work as the material. The leader should have a knowledge of dance and movement meditation techniques (modern dance and yoga are most helpful), a familiarity with Scripture and prayer, a commitment to peace and an ability to work with groups. Leading the workshops can be done by an individual or a team. The team could include a religious educator, a dancer or movement specialist, and a peacemaker.

Establishing the workshop climate

Workshops are most productive when people feel congenial and trusting. It is important to create a nonjudgmental, noncompetitive, exploratory atmosphere. Most people are hesitant to let their bodies express their feelings, positively or negatively, especially if they feel threatened. Some are conditioned by early taboos about the body, which are not easily overcome. Some shy away from personal movement while still others think of dance only as an art form rather than a natural form of expression available to all.

The leader can foster a nonthreatening transition from past fears to present trust. The key is to be natural, unassuming, and open. The leader's role is to create the appropriate combination of space and silence so that each person can connect more deeply with his/her own responses and insights. The leader must also determine the proper amounts of freedom and structure for each group. In the context of a communal experience, the sharing can be truly sacramental.

Understanding the general philosophy of the workshops

PeaceRites assumes the whole is more than the sum of its parts and the entire dance experience is built by each individual, one by one; a reflecting, dancing community becomes effective in proportion to the growth and development of each individual in it; the desire of people to be peacemakers is strengthened and encouraged by effective participation in workshops and rites that are well planned; peacemaking engages every level of an individual; inspiration comes from many sources, including ecumenical and interfaith insights that have a universal application.

Preparing the physical environment

Choose a large, uncluttered room for the sessions with a wood floor, if possible. The surroundings should be peaceful and beautiful. The room should have a central focus for meditation, e.g., a candle or flower arrangement to enhance the opening prayer.

Workshop materials

- a good quality cassette tape recorder;
- the recommended music tapes, and artifacts;
- any supplemental material, such as additional pictures of oppressed peoples or endangered animals, favorite quotes on peace, special prayers.

Recommended clothing

Participants should wear dance/exercise clothes, i.e., loose fitting garments that are comfortable to move in.

Organizing time

Each workshop unit is designed for a half-day, about three hours, with suggested time allotments as follows:

- INTRODUCTION TO THE THEME (20 minutes);
- INVOCATION (5-10 minutes);
- WARM-UP (30 minutes);
- THEME WORK (30 minutes);
- BREAK (15 minutes);
- STUDY (40 minutes);
- PREPARATION FOR RITE OR CONCLUDING DANCE (15 minutes);
- CLOSING RITE (20 minutes).

The Warm-Up

Introduction

The purpose of the warm-up is to awaken the movement potential within each one of us by sensitizing ourselves to our bodies, stretching and loosening our limbs and muscles. The work addresses the physical dimension of our bodies, helping us through movement discover our inner harmony and responsiveness to life. Integral to this method is the affirmation that each of us is a complex and unique person. We do not all move and look alike. Therefore, we do not compare ourselves with anyone else. Our purpose is to discover something about ourselves. We will not judge ourselves by ballet or modern dance aesthetic standards.

The warm-up asks for full concentration and a working attitude toward our bodies. Much can be discovered by moving a little farther in a stretch than is immediately comfortable, or by daring to go fully into a movement idea that is unfamiliar. Try not to be concerned about the expectations of others but respond from within with an easy attitude.

The warm-up is included to assist leaders with little dance experience. If a dancer is on the team, they should feel free to glance at the material and shape it their own way.

Preparation

Please stand. Spread out around the room. To make sure you are not too close to anyone, open your arms wide and check that you have enough room to move about.

Close your eyes. Feel your feet on the floor. They are your main source of support. Strength and connectedness can be enhanced from the way you stand.

7

Sense the length of your spine, from the top of your head to your "tail-bone" (lowest vertebra). Feel your spine long, your head lifting out of your neck, your neck lifting from your shoulders, your shoulders hanging easily, chest open, stomach lifted, rib cage lowered downward. Your lower back is relaxed and long.

With your eyes still closed, check your body for any tension. Relax the muscles of the face, neck, shoulders, arms, ribs, spine, pelvis, legs, feet. Your body should be at ease, yet alert and awake. Breathe slowly . . . in . . . and out . . . in . . . and out. Each time you breathe out, release any worry or fatigue. Let it drop away from you. Imagine refreshing water flowing over you, then draining off into the floor. As you breathe, feel a sense of warmth filling your chest, your heart, and your whole body.

Stretching

Reach upward, lifting your arms overhead, stretching from the bottom of your feet to the tips of your fingers. Your head is lifted, your spine long, ribs down, as if flat against your back. Maintaining the stretch, reach straight forward with your body. Imagine the distance between your vertebrae lengthening. Bend your knees and lower your body, bringing your head toward your knees and curving your spine so you are like a little ball. Breathe in deeply in this position. Breathe out, and slowly uncurl your spine, feeling your weight dropping to the floor as you rise, standing with your arms down at your sides, your chest open. Pause a moment, and be aware of yourself, in all simplicity.

Be conscious of your alignment. Check that your shoulders are vertically aligned with your hips. We will repeat the stretch once again. Reach upward with your arms, head lifted, hands open. Be sure your ribs are down. Reach forward, as far as you can, out into space, stretching your spine. Bend your knees and drop over, your tail-bone down, your head folded in toward your knees. Breathe in, feeling your lower back expand; then breathing out, slowly straighten up, this time with your arms reaching up overhead.

Extend your arms on either side and place your legs apart, with your feet facing forward and your knees aligned with your toes. Bending your knees, squat down and round your body over, placing your hands on the floor between your feet. Your head should be low, almost between your legs. Bring your head to your right knee. Straighten your right knee, keeping your head close to your knee. Bend the right knee, and with your body still rounded over, move to your left side.

Bring your head to your left knee, and straighten it, with your body as before. Bend both knees. Return your head to your right knee. Straighten the right knee and bring your right arm back (in this position it will be overhead), look back toward your right hand stretching from your fingertips all the way down your spine. Look back toward your right hand. Center yourself between your legs, body rounded over repeat on the left, reaching overhead and back with your left arm as you straighten your left leg. Look back toward your left hand. Bend both legs and uncurl your back as you return to a standing position.

Swings

Bring both feet together and reach overhead with your arms. In slow motion, bend your knees as your arms swing forward and down. Straighten your knees as your arms continue the momentum of the swing backward. Bend your knees as your arms move forward, and straighten them as your arms lift overhead. Adding the torso, bend your knees as your body drops and rounds over; then straighten your knees with your head still down and arms back. Bend your knees and straighten as you swing upward. All together, a little faster, swinging down . . . and up, down . . . and up, down . . . and up, down . . . and up, letting go, feeling the natural momentum. When you reach upward, keep the movement flowing, never stopping, moving beyond your fingers and out into space. Down . . . and up, lift . . . and drop.

The following movements are in preparation for the side swings, so that your back will be strengthened and you will feel centered. Extend your arms to the side with feet apart. Your back should feel free, not pinched. Your feet are turned slightly outward. Cup your hands in front of your heart, like an opening flower. Reach with your arms and torso to the right. Return to your center, hands in the cupped position. Reach to the left, and return to your center.

When you swing, your arms will come down as you pass through your center. Swing to the right, release your arms down, and then swing to the left . . . right . . . left . . . right . . . left . . . right . . . left, each time with a "fall and rebound" quality to the swing.

Now with greater momentum, bend your knees and round your body over each time as you swing from right to left, like a pendulum moving from side to side. Repeat four times: right . . . left . . . right . . . left . . . right . . . left . . . right . . . left. Extend your arms on either side. Feel the movement energy running from the center of your back outward, beyond your hands, with your heart open and your arms like rays of the sun.

Stretching the Spine

Bring your legs together. Curving your spine to the right, bend both knees and in a squatting position, wrap your arms clockwise around your body, your left arm in front, your right arm in back, looking back over your right shoulder. Extend your arms on either side and repeat the wrapping movement counter clockwise.

The Warm-Up

Again to the right, and to the left, each time extend your arms wider and twisting side to side with more momentum. Wrap and twist to the right, stretch your arms out, and wrap and twist to the left, to the right . . . to the left . . . lift . . . drop, . . . lift . . . drop. Return to center. Extend your arms sideways. Feel the movement energy running horizontally and vertically: sideways, downward, beyond your feet, and upward beyond your head. Hold.

Arm Swings

Start with your arms stretched to the sides. With a circular motion swing them down and cross them in front of you. Lift them over head and open them upward and sideways, like an arc. Repeat. Drop down . . . then up and open to the sides, drop . . . lift..and open, drop . . . lift . . . and open. Reverse the movement, lifting upward, crossing your arms in front of you as they swing down and rebound upward on either side. Lift up, cross your arms, and swing down and back up on either side (4 times). (The leader may add any swings, such as forward and backward, like a pinwheel, or even free-form. She/he can combine this with moving forward and backward and sideways in space.)

Floor Stretches

Sit on the floor in a comfortable, cross-legged position, spine erect, arms at your sides. Breathe in deeply, feeling your lungs expand, and slowly breathe out. Your spine is straight, stomach lifted, ribs lowered.

Round over to the front, 1 . . . 2 . . . 3 . . . 4; then straighten your spine, unfolding upward 1 . . . 2 . . . 3 . . . 4: back to your centered position. Now curve backward, rounding your spine 1 . . . 2 . . . 3 . . . 4, and lifting 1 . . . 2 . . . 3 . . . 4. Let's repeat, rounding forward . . . lifting . . . curving backward . . . and straightening back to center. Turn to your right. Place both hands on the floor and bend your body over to the right knee, lift up, and repeat to the left. Keep both hips on the floor. Repeat to the right . . . and to the left.

Cup both hands in front of you, breath in, bring both knees in front of you, breathe out, and lower your back to the floor. Straighten your legs out and come to a complete stretch—your toes pointed, your back long, your arms reaching over your head. You are in one long line from your fingertips to your toes. Your ribs are down, and the space between your lower back and the floor is minimum. Stretch lengthwise in both directions at once.

Bend your knees up, feet on the floor near your buttocks; raise your head and shoulders, holding onto the back of your thighs, and curl your spine up, 1 . . . 2 . . . 3 . . . 4, your head coming close to your knees; then straighten your back vertically. Roll back down to the floor for 4 counts. Repeat.

Lying on your back, bring your knees to your chest. With your arms extended on either side, let your knees fall to the right, feel the stretch through your whole spine, return to center and drop to the left. Repeat. (By swinging your knees from side to side, any stiffness in the lower spine is worked out.) Raise your head to your knees and roll down from the back, keeping your knees to your chest.

Plow and Shoulder Stand

Roll backward into the "plow" position. (In the plow, your weight is on your neck, shoulders and upper back. Your legs are bent by on each side of your head). Remain in this position for one minute. If your back hurts, ease yourself down and rest with your knees to your chest. Support your back with your hands and rise up into the shoulder stand. Reach with your legs to the ceiling. Feel the movement traveling beyond your feet, upward. Hold for a minute. Lower both legs to the floor behind you, flex or point your feet, and carefully roll down your spine until you are resting on the floor, your knees on your chest or pointed upward, feet on the floor close to your buttocks. Rest.

Forward Stretch

From the previous position lift your head, reach forward with your hands and take hold of your thighs. Curl upward to a sitting position. Extend your legs straight out in front of you.

Reach upward with your hands, flex your feet (toes back, heels forward), and extend your torso forward, stretching horizontally parallel to your legs, your head between your arms. Breathe in...and out, reaching forward a little more with each breath. Release and let your body rest.

Back Arch

Roll over onto your stomach, legs stretched out behind you. Place your hands, palms down, under your shoulders, your forehead on the floor. Pressing gently on your hands, slowly arch your spine by first lifting your head and extending your neck. Continue stretching forward, upward, and backward. Hold for eight counts. Lower your torso, feeling first your stomach against the floor, then your ribs, chest and finally your head. Rest. Repeat.

If your body is ready, bend your knees and take hold of your ankles. Stretch in this position. Breathe in deeply. Breathe out as you lift up, pressing your chest forward, and knees upward. Hold . . . and lower your body back to the floor. Press your hands against the floor, raise your back and pull yourself backward from the hips and spine until you are sitting on your heels. Curl your upper body into a ball, with your head resting on the floor. Clasp your hands behind your back. Relax your spine. Uncurl and sit back on your heels, arms at your sides.

Free Stretch

Everyone's body has particular needs. This is a time to stretch on the floor in any way you like and see how freely you can move on your back, sides, stomach, and knees, while working out any other tensions, thus freeing and loosening your body. Move continuously. Reach in any direction . . . stretch like a cat . . . curl your arms and legs . . . wiggle your spine . . . stretch your facial muscles, including your eyes, nose, and mouth . . . flex your fingers and wrists, circle your arms . . . lift your shoulders. Just let go and roll . . . forward . . . and backward, loosening up every-thing. Shake your hands, arms, flop around, stretch out . . . and relax.

The leader may also encourage the group to make sounds as they stretch. This can be very helpful, especially if it prompts people to laugh and relax.

Moving in Space

We will now add the dimension of moving in space, around the floor. Please stand. You may move in any direction you like, in a "milling about" fashion. Sense what is happening with your whole body, as if you had "eyes" all over.

We will begin by walking. Walk in a clean crisp way. Feel your feet firmly on the floor and be aware of each step you take. Mill around, passing others, without looking directly at anybody and yet taking everybody in as well as the intervening space. Notice your distance from or nearness to the people around you. Continue walking, altering your pace as you wish, then add movement with your arms . . . and torso.

Reach out with your arms, playing with space. Bend your body as you move, curving in circles, turning around, moving arms, ribs, chest, hips, knees. It is as if you are walking over the surface of the earth . . . moving freely as a child.

Now let's move at a *much slower pace*. Slow down and be even more conscious of your feet in contact with the floor. Every step can be meaningful. Gradually move closer to one another: How does this feel? Gradually move apart: How does this feel? Pause. Reach toward someone far away from you. They don't have to be looking at you. They can be looking at someone else. The main thing is for you to discover how you can connect with them across space.

Lower your arm and this time reach toward someone near you. Lower your arm and reach toward someone far away . . . toward someone a little closer . . . and toward someone very near you. Lower your arm.

Exploring Space

Standing in one area, explore movements very close to you, that are in your *personal space*. You are absorbed in close, intimate movements . . . Without stopping, gradually increase your range of movement and explore the space beyond your personal sphere, with further extensions of your arms, legs, torso. You can now move a small distance around yourself. Slowly circle and extend your arms outward, farther and farther away from your torso, until you are reaching out into space: imagine that your spirit extends beyond the boundaries of walls. We are becoming aware of, exploring, and growing comfortable with movements close to our body, movements further away, and movements that extend far outward.

Changing tempo, walk faster and faster and break into a run. Pass one another, still conscious of your feet on the floor. You are now comfortable with moving in space. Play with it! Move around one another, relate to each other as you pass by . . . turning and jumping. Changing tempo again, start to slow down, gradually coming to a stop. Pause.

Reach once again toward someone far away; lower your arm and reach toward someone close to you, and this time physically connect. Clasp hands, or touch a shoulder. Stay connected and reach toward another person and also connect. Adjust in such a way that everyone in the room is eventually linked in an interlocking web of mutual support. Holding on, slowly *lean* forward or backward feeling the support. Slowly sway, carefully shifting your weight as need be, so that the whole group is a living, pulsing unit . . . and slowly return to your own center of weight. Release your hands, let go . . . and stand quietly. Feel connected to everyone in the room . . . through your feet . . . through your heart . . . through your entire body.

The Warm-Up

WORKSHOP I

Disarming the Self

Introduction to the Theme

Etty Hillesum, a young woman who died in the concentration camps in World War II, wrote while imprisoned, "Ultimately, we have just one moral duty: to reclaim large areas of peace in ourselves, more and more peace, and to reflect it toward others. And the more peace in us, the more peace there will also be in our troubled world."

An Interrupted Life, The Diaries of Etty Hillesum 1941-43, Washington Square Press, 1981, p. 229.

This is the first of the workshops which explore peace through movement. We begin with searching inwardly to uncover the roots of conflict in ourselves. As we face them, we begin the disarming process in our hearts. This process requires inner prayer, a focusing on self-awareness and watchfulness. With humility we turn to God for strength and wisdom.

Through our acceptance of our unique journey and our struggles on the road to inner peace, we can hopefully begin to face our own defenses and armaments. These wall us off from accepting our strengths and working with our inner struggles and conflicts. If we delve within, we do not blame or point the finger to *outer* demons. Mahatma Gandhi reminds us, "The only demons are those warring in our own hearts and that's where the battles should be fought. Similarly, Jesus asked, "Why do you observe the splinter in your brother's eye and never notice the plank in you own? . . . Take the plank out of your own eye first, and then you will see clearly enough to take the splinter out of your neighbor's eye."

Cf. *Gandhi*, directed by Richard Attenborough.

Matthew 7:3-5.

Peace in our hearts and the overcoming of anxiousness and fear are closely related. Through fear of facing difficult situations, we encase ourselves in a protective armor that is rigid and even self-righteous. When fear is overcome, we respond and

17

act closer to "our real selves." When we are released from inner bondage, we feel a new freshness, as in spring, when warm air and sunlight touch our skin after a long winter. This release is like a smile that arises spontaneously from the heart: a "thank you" for a new awareness of inner and outer unity.

At its core, the heart is pure, flowing love. This workshop concerns facing the forces that bind us and prevent us loving. From this perspective, it is not the heart that needs to be disarmed, but our personal attitudes. In this workshop we may discern how and when our feelings/actions toward others are distorted by our personal fears and needs. We become more conscious of our projections. The process aids us in making our own "rough paths smooth," preparing ourselves to become peacemakers in a troubled world.

I am reminded of a friend who continually seems to act before thinking, appears imprudent with money, doesn't plan ahead, and repeatedly entangles herself in dissatisfying personal relationships. She seemed enmeshed in crises which emerge periodically both for herself and her children. I often found judgmental attitudes, anger, and frustration arising within me. In analyzing this situation, I recognized that while it might seem appropriate to blame the person, there were hidden issues involved. By looking deeper and learning what was going on in my own heart, I was able to understand the difference between the anger I projected and the appropriate response. I learned to set my own boundaries and yet remain loving.

If I can discern in one situation something about my own nature with the unwitting "help" of another, I will have moved a step ahead toward taking the "plank out of my own eye," and truly act with love and forgiveness. This insight is a crucial element to peacemaking. By learning from this instance, I am better equipped to examine more complex situations.

Giving expression to this process through movement is a wonderful fresh approach toward a new understanding of peace-making. By paying attention to the non-verbal, angers and frustrations can be released from the body. So often they seem to be repressed.

Let us now turn to the "armaments," the focus of this workshop.

Armaments

The leader draws the group into a discussion of personal "armaments." What do we mean by "armaments"? Generally this term refers to the various ways in which people lock themselves up to avoid feelings or actions that have been associated with pain or pleasure in the past. Some armaments or defenses are very rigid and may be beyond a person's reach without professional thera-peutic guidance. In this workshop we seek to acknowledge these older defenses and open new pathways for feeling, in an accepting atmosphere. We are not seeking to achieve the changes which can occur in analysis or inner states of contemplation. The workshop offers a vehicle which aligns people with their common yearning for peace on earth. The leader opens this section by directing the group in a general discussion of real or imagined "enemies" against which we build protection. The group may discuss various ways they avoid commitment or involvement, such as:

blaming others (projection)	"You (they) make me act or feel this way." Focusing on faults of others when we are unwilling to face what is going on within us.
above it all (detachment)	"I am not like them. I'm above it all or better than . . . " etc. "I won't take sides" no matter what the situation (being a peace-makers means being involved).
too busy (avoidance) and escapism . . . (the flight from reality).	I'll change the subject, go to the bathroom, play music, drink, so I won't feel anything new (I'll get away from "it all," watch TV, attend church).
turning the blame on oneself (being a martyr)	"It's all my fault," despite objective evidence to the contrary (self-punishment instead of self-surrender, self-pity instead of self-concern).
shifting responsibility /displacements	"I'm too tired to handle this.
rigidity	"It's better to be safe than sorry."
addiction	Use of chocolate, coffee, alcohol, sweets or drugs when upset . . . rather than facing the issue at hand.
denial	"I never do that or feel (that) way . . ." "I never hate anyone."

Other suggestions proposed may include overcompetence, intellectualizing, and passivity. The leader encourages the group to name these and/or other defense mechanisms that we recognize in ourselves, and explains that they will be explored further as part of the study.

Invocation

Preparation: Place a candle in a central position. Ask all to sit cross-legged or in a comfortable, but prayerful, position.

We come together in meditation. We focus our minds and hearts, and pray, stilling our inner and outer selves, opening ourselves to receive grace and the insight needed for spiritual growth. Slowly breathe . . . in and out . . . Feel connected to the candle. (Pause) Bring the light into your heart, the center of your being. (The leader may reach out to the candle and then bring her hands toward her body, as if drawing the fire to herself. Some may naturally follow and imitate this gesture.) Fire gives warmth and energy. Fire also purifies, transforms. Feel the warmth and light enter into every part of your being. Reach with your hands toward the fire . . . a gesture from the dawn of time. (Hands return to rest at sides or in lap.) We will meditate for a few minutes with Psalm 139—a very personal psalm. The psalmist cries, "O God you know my most intimate self," and seems to be implying, help me to know myself, to be as aware of myself as you are of me. To be aware of ourselves is the foundation of our work on personal disarmament. Now listen, letting the following words enter into your being. Listen with your mind and body in prayer.

O God, you search me and know me!
You know when I sit down and when I rise up;
you discern my thoughts from afar . . .
Where shall I go from thy Spirit?
Or where shall I flee from thy presence?
If I ascend to heaven you are there!
If I make my bed in Sheol, you are there . . .
If I say, "Let only darkness cover me,
and the light about me be night,"
even the darkness is not dark to you,
the night is bright as the day;
for darkness is as light with you.
For you have formed my inward parts,
you knit me together in my mother's womb . . .
     Search me, O God, and know my heart!
Try me and know my thoughts!
And see if there be any wicked way in me,
and lead me in the way everlasting.

The leader prays:

Spirit of the universe, forgive us for any harm we have done to ourselves, to other living creatures and to our environment. May we be guided in our inner search, exploring the ways that make for peace.

May peace be in my mind, on my lips, and in my heart.

The prayer concludes with a gesture. Bring your hands together, palm to palm. Focus your energy and slowly touch your forehead, lips and heart. Cross your arms over your chest and fold into a reverent bow from the waist. Hold for a moment and gradually unfold. Moving from the heart, slowly reach out your arms as if to touch all people, visualizing linking your heart to all living beings. Greet your neighbors.

Theme Work

Naming and dancing a personal "armament."

To help us find a physical channel for dancing our "armaments," we turn to the dance technique of isolation. Isolation explores the movement potential of a particular part of the body. Isolating parts of the body, one at a time, also allows us to discover the emotional richness that each part of the body can express.

The Head

Drop your head forward . . . backward . . . sideways to the right . . . to the left. Repeat. Move in a complete circle (forward . . . roll to the right, backward . . . roll to the left). Reverse . . . and repeat, circling to the right . . . and to the left. Turn your head, looking to the right . . . and to the left. Look in all different directions . . . sharply as if alert to danger . . . then slowly, with a sense of awe. Improvise movements of the head that express anger . . . arrogance . . . shame . . . questioning. (The leader may suggest adding a hand or arm movement to help increase the expressive quality.)

Let your head gradually *lead* the rest of your body as we add the dimension of space. Change levels . . . alternating between sinking to the floor and back up, and moving about in space. Note that the head is still initiating the movements. Gather together to one side of the room and choose an emotion such as pride, anger, fear or shame. Dance that feeling, leading with the head, while moving to the other side of the room . . . You may crawl, run, turn, or move in any way that you can devise. (Variation: The entire group moves, with the same emotion.)

We will continue in a similar fashion as described for the head, isolating shoulders and elbows, chest, hips and pelvis, knees, and feet.

The Shoulders and Elbows

Lift your shoulders up and down, up and down. Circle the shoulders . . . forward, up, back and down. Repeat. Reverse the circle. Bring your hands to your shoulders and circle your elbows . . . forward, up, back, and down. Repeat. Reverse the circle. Thrust the elbows forward, lifting the chest. Thrust the elbows backward, curving the chest forward. Move your arms in many directions, exploring the flow of movement from shoulders, to elbows, to ribs, to chest and torso. Move with different qualities— soft feelings, liquid movements, slowly being pulled in different directions. Add feelings to these movements such as fearfulness, yearning, anger. Move in space as we did with the head, but with the shoulders, then elbows, then arms initiating the movement. Gather together on one side of the room, and as before, choose an

Workshop I

emotion and dance that feeling, leading with the shoulders and elbows while moving to the other side of the room.

The Chest

Wrap your arms around your chest and curve forward. Experience how you feel with your chest huddled inward. Release your arms and expand your chest at the same time; feel as if you are opening to the whole world. Repeat this a few times, closing in . . . releasing . . . starting the movement with the chest contracted and then expanding. Circle your chest . . . forward, sideways, backward, to the other side. Reverse the circle. Repeat, sensing what it feels like when you circle this way. Add your breath. Breathe in and out, in different rhythms, as you curve inward, expand outward, circle around. Play with this while changing the quality of the movement. Move lightly, in a sustained way . . . with soft impulses . . . now heavily as if sobbing . . . now as if nurturing, with steadiness and flow. As before, move in space, leading with your chest, with a feeling of grief, or pride, or ecstasy, or control. Choose one of these emotions and move across the room.

The Hips, Pelvis and Knees

Begin by moving your hips forward, backward, side to side. Circle to the right . . . and to the left. Try these movements in combination with the pelvis and knees. Move them in a sensuous way . . . now sharply with accents, thrusting in different directions. Do this with a feeling of playfulness, suggestiveness, anger, and tenderness. As before, move around the room, leading with your hips, pelvis and knees, choosing an emotion as a motivating force. Now all come to one side of the room and move across to the other, leading with either the hips, pelvis or knees. Choose an emotion as you do so.

The Feet

Shift your weight slowly, forward and backward, feeling your feet on the floor . . . Curl your toes, flex them . . . curl . . . flex. Move your feet in different directions, standing on one leg and then the other, circling your ankle, shaking your feet . . . turning in and out . . . tapping lightly, pointing, jumping. Play with different rhythms, moving as if your feet had a mind of their own. Move around yourself in different directions, as if you were in a great indecision: Which way should you go? Stop. Now let's all go to one side of the room and move across it, choosing one emotion and expressing it through the feet.

Body Weight

In preparation for the study, participants need to be comfortable moving in a one-to-one relationship that uses the other person's weight and physical energy.

Please take partners. Extend your right hand and clasp your partner's hand. Lean back in opposite directions and feel how you can mutually support one another. Change hands. Repeat. Now try leaning in different directions, experimenting with your weight and the different shapes your bodies can take. Clasp both hands and lower toward the floor. Rise together, still holding on. Taking right hands, pull in opposition to one another, as if in a hand-to-hand battle. Experiment moving in space, forward and backward and sideways.

Isolation in Small Groups

This study is not essential, but helpful. It allows the participants to further their experience dancing with others, learning to react and "bounce off" one another's energies. Divide into groups of threes and fours. Suggest one of the armaments discussed in the Introduction, such as "Blaming others", assign a body part (e.g., fingers, shoulders) and have the groups interact, everyone "blaming" the others in their group. For "above it all," you might suggest movement initiated by the chest, with the emotion of arrogance. Don't be surprised if the study evokes laughter, releasing built-up anxiety.

Dancing a Personal Armament

Ask the participants to find their own "private place" in the room. Their task is to focus on one of their own "armaments" and discover movements that express it. It may be helpful to recall an incident in your life that touched off an exaggerated emotional response. Picture and recall the feelings of your reactions and the other people involved. (When you feel attacked, how do you defend yourself?) Take time after the study to reflect on the use of the armament in relation to the incident.

These "armament movements" should be strong, simple, clear, and teachable—not sequential dance movement, but images that express an inner state. Recalling the isolation exercises will be helpful.

Some people may choose to start with movement first, in an unprogrammed way, and discern from the movement something about the armament. Others may first need a period of quiet, to move from inner understanding to outer expression. The success of the study is dependent upon the accuracy of each person's pattern in reflecting an armament that plays a significant role in real life. The dance pattern need not be literal, but must be truly expressive of some aspect of the armament. For example, let's say the armament concerns avoidance, running away. The person's pattern might include a turning away of the head, hand shielding his eyes, feet moving backwards. But that movement might be "right on" for one person, and not right for another. It has to feel right from the guts. Remember, too, the body is being asked to express outwardly what is normally not expressed. The movements reflect inner actions, movements of the emotions and spirit.

Study: Wrestling with an Angel

Reading the Scriptural Text

Genesis 27-34, paraphrased
by Ann Doemland.

Call the group together. In the context of the biblical account of Jacob wrestling with the angel we have a deeply moving story of one man who "wrestles all night," and we find here a model for our own work.

Jacob had always lived by his wits. At birth he was the second twin, but he came out of the womb grasping his brother's heel and was named Jacob, which means "he takes by the heel" or "he supplants." As a young man he bargained with his brother Esau for the birthright of the firstborn. Once when Esau came in from hunting, famished and empty-handed, Jacob was making lentil soup (the famous "mess of pottage" in the language of the King James Version). Esau was dying of hunger, but Jacob would only barter food in exchange for Esau's birthright.

What counted most, however, was the blessing that only their father, Isaac, could give. To steal the blessing required an elaborate scheme, which was dreamed up and encouraged by their mother, Rebekah. When Isaac, old and blind, asked Esau to go hunting and prepare his favorite dish, Rebekah quickly cooked a goat to his liking. Since Esau was hairy and Jacob was smooth-skinned, she dressed Jacob in his brother's clothes and covered his hands and neck with the skin of the goat. When Jacob went in to Isaac, the blind old man was confused by the voice, but trusted his other senses—the taste of the food, the smell of Esau's clothes, the hairy hands. And he gave his powerful and irreversible blessing to the imposter.

Needless to say, Esau was angry and muttered that his father could not live much longer. Then he would feel free to kill his supplanter. Jacob, in fear, fled to the land where his uncle Laban, his mother's brother, lived. Here he encountered someone just as tricky as himself. He worked seven years to earn the hand of his uncle's daughter, Rachel, but in the dark of the wedding night Laban substituted his older daughter Leah. After another seven years of work for Rachel, Jacob entered into an elaborate agreement with Laban as to which part of the flocks Jacob would henceforth earn as pay. Cheating and countercheating ensued, but finally Jacob succeeded in building up so much wealth that Laban's sons became envious.

So Jacob gathered together his wives, children, servants, and flocks and fled back toward the land of his birth. But as he drew near to Canaan, he learned that Esau had heard of his approach and was coming to meet him with four hundred men. Old fears came back to him. He did what he could, but his wits would not get him out of this one. He sent on ahead elaborate presents to Esau. He divided his family, followers, and flock into two groups, which would travel different routes so that if one group was attacked the other would still be saved. But what of himself?

At this point, ask someone to read Genesis 32:22-29 and 33:1-4. Then say: It was not by chance that there was no need for the anticipated battle with Esau. Jacob had fought his own inner battle all night long. He was a changed man. He was no longer "the Supplanter," but Israel, "the One Who Strives with God."

Preparing for the Study

We are now ready to dance a personalized version of *Jacob Wrestling with the Angel*. Each person will have a chance to play Jacob, and also the angel. When you play Jacob, the dance will enable you to experience in a unique way your own armament, or shield, through the angel's interpretation of it. You see your own pattern reflected back to you. We do not know how Jacob fought with the angel, but we do know the outcome. He was changed. His real self emerged. (But he was also wounded, in the thigh, a vulnerable place. What needs to be wounded in you, or what is wounded and needs a blessing?) Likewise, dancing in confrontation with one of your own armaments, and being blessed in the bargain, can also be one step toward freeing your real self.

Dancing this confrontation will lead to a release from the blind power of the armament over you. To dance with an "enemy" is to transform the battle into play. The dance ends in victory, for it ends with a blessing. Your own armament, personified by the angel, blesses you. It is fitting, for by dancing with it you will be lead to greater self-understanding. And, like Jacob, after confronting and fighting your own inner battle, the outer world will be changed. You are on the way to being a peacemaker. One student remarked, "When we name our demons, they become angels!"

The Dance

Choose partners. Designate one person as A (ANGEL) and the other as J (JACOB). Person JACOB teaches his ANGEL partner the J armament movements. This is the key, for we are to confront our own armament! JACOB wrestles with his own armament which is visible in the movements of Person ANGEL.

When all are ready, the JACOBS lie on the floor, asleep, as in the story. The ANGELS stand near their partners. When the music begins, the JACOBS wake up and begin wrestling with the ANGELS who are dancing the taught armament. (Urge the ANGELS to maintain their partner's armament patterns with all their strength. Instruct the JACOBS that they are impelled to confront the angel.) Jacob said to the angel, "I will not let you go, unless you bless me." After a period of time, partners should move into a final confrontation, which in turn leads to the blessing. Who blesses whom? In the story the angel blesses Jacob. In the dance, which portrays a confrontation with ourselves, either person may bless.

Who is this angel who had been sent to help Jacob? While in Jerusalem in 1990, I asked a lecturer from an Israeli peace organization. He stated that according to Jewish mysticism, Jacob wrestled with **Esau's guardian angel**! It may be that

Workshop I

Laurens Van der Post suggests that the story of Jacob and Esau represents a fundamental, deep divide in the psychology and history of the human race—that of the hunter, without property, and that of the husbandman, who wins, apparently even the favor of God. Is not this war, this divide, overcome in Jesus, dancing his love for all, on the cross? Esau's opening his arms to Jacob may be a neglected, but important part of the Scripture to be danced. (Van der Post, *A Mantis Carol*, Island Press, 1975, p. 102.)

during the night, Jacob was helped not only to confront his misdeeds, and understand and master them, but also to atone for them through the wound inflicted by the angel. At the beginning of the story, we see Jacob stealing the birthright blessing from Esau. Now Jacob is wrestling another blessing and Esau is involved—through his guardian angel. How mysteriously we assist in one another's growth. Was the angel sent only to protect Esau? Had Esau already forgiven Jacob, and, in love, sent his inner angel? We can only conjecture and learn. Perhaps all our inner struggles can be seen as gifts from God, offering blessings and growth.

Before any discussion, reverse roles, and repeat the whole process of teaching the armament, wrestling, and blessing. When each pair is finished, they may quietly discuss together all that has happened. When all have finished, invite the group as a whole to reflect on their experiences.

It will help to experience the study as a "dance" if each pair finds an opening position, as the angel and Jacob, before beginning, and at the end holds for a moment the final blessing, or closing position.

Rite

The Opening

Place the candle from the "Invocation" in a central position on the floor. Ask all to gather around it, sitting in a meditative position.

The leader says: We come together in support and prayer as we acknowledge our brokenness and fragmentation. We seek the healing and blessing and counsel of the Spirit to strengthen us. We are not defenseless, nor defined by our brokenness or wounds. St. Paul writes to the Ephesians: "Put on the whole armor of God . . . stand therefore, having girded your loins with truth, and having put on the breastplate of righteousness, and having shod your feet with the equipment of the gospel of peace."

We come together in prayer, thankful for what we have experienced and shared:

> *Let the light of the flame reflect your own inner light.*
> *The "armor" of God comes from within and radiates outward,*
> *breaking down the walls of rigid boundaries,*
> *releasing us to love.*
> *We ask to be strengthened by our inner light,*
> *to be opened by grace, through the movement of the spirit.*

The Reading

"The practice of contemplative prayer is especially valuable for advancing harmony and peace in the world. For this prayer rises, by divine grace, where there is total disarmament of the heart and unfolds in an experience of love which is the moving force of peace. Contemplation fosters a vision of the human family as united and interdependent in the mystery of God's love for all people. This silent, interior prayer bridges temporarily the 'already' and 'not yet,' this world and God's kingdom of peace." (Allow a few minutes for silence.)

The Challenge of Peace: God's Promise and Our Response, National Conference of Catholic Bishops, 1983, #294.

Preparation for Peace Dance

The unlit candles are distributed to each participant, and three concentric circles are formed. One person holds a globe or symbol of the world in the center. A light is passed, from one person to the next, until everybody's candle is lit.

The leader says: Let us have the courage to believe in a bright future and in a God who wills it for us—not a perfect world, but a better one . . . a better world is here for human hands and hearts and minds to make.

Ibid., #337, excerpt.

The rite is concluded by a circle dance for peace, to either *Dona Nobis Pacem*, or *Peace Is Flowing Like a River*, whichever song is more familiar to the group.

Peace Dance

Dona Nobis Pacem is a beautiful and well-known song that can be sung as a three-part canon. All sing it first in unison, standing in the three concentric circles, facing center and the globe of the earth. Then the innermost circle begins singing, walking counterclockwise. The middle circle comes in after the second *Dona nobis pacem*, and circles clockwise. The third circle enters in turn, circling counterclockwise. The canon is repeated at least three times. On the last round each circle ends facing inward, toward the globe. All candles are lifted in unison.

Peace Is Flowing Like a River is performed in the same manner as above, except that it is not done as a canon. Participants can suggest alternate words for each stanza, e.g., **peace** is flowing like a river, or **love** is flowing like a river, etc.

>>>>>

WORKSHOP MATERIALS

Listed below are the materials and music for Workshop I. The leader may wish to substitute music according to availability. Care should be taken to match the feeling and tone of the suggestions. The leader may work in silence, and/or with live accompaniment.

Invocation

Materials:	Candle
Music:	Meditative, quiet
	James Galway plays Songs of the Sea shore and other Melodies of Japan.
	Cathedral Pines from *New Friend*, Eugene Friesen with Paul Halley, Living Music Records
	Sunsinger, Paul Winter, Living Music Records
	Amazing Grace from *Datura*, Susan Osborn, Lifeline Recordings, PO Box 848, Eastsound, WA 98245

Warm-Up

Materials:	Drum or rhythm instrument
Music:	Quiet, moving to flowing and joyous
	December, George Winston, Windham Hill Recordings
	The Mission, Sound Track, Ennio Morriane, Virgin Records
	Sunsinger, Paul Winter, Living Music Records

Theme Work

Music:	Rhythmic
	Drumming, Steve Reich, Nonesuch
	Live accompaniment

Study

Music:	Dramatic, soul-searching
	Ignacio from *Entends tu Les Chiens Aboyer?*, Vangelis, Barclay Recordings
	Mystical Adventures (Part V), Jean Luc Ponty, Atlantic
	Sockdolager from *Canyon*, Paul Winter, Living Music
	Sea Storm from *Callings*, Paul Winter, Living Music
	Glassworks, Philip Glass

Rite

Materials:	Candle for each participant and globe, or symbol of the world
Music:	*Dona Nobis Pacem*
	Peace Is Flowing Like A River

WORKSHOP II

In Touch with Others

Introduction to the Theme

Even though it was many years ago, I still recall serving a particular meal at the New York City Catholic Worker soup kitchen. I remember because it felt like a dance in slow motion. As I served, I walked slowly, gently, bowing deeply within, smiling with a sense of simplicity guiding my actions. I felt thread-like connections to the hungry men and women who came in to the dining room. I treasure the experience. "The body is one and has many members, and all the members of the body, though many, are one body . . . if one member suffers, all suffer together; if one member is honored, all rejoice together." (1 Corinthians 12:12, 26).

How can we come to feel with every fiber of our being the words of St. Paul? How can we respond in our hearts to the cries and laughter of all beings? We experience troubling contradictions in our personal and social lives which make it difficult for us to focus on the foundation of love of which Paul speaks and to shape our lives by this vision of unity. On the one hand, we are impressed by the selfless work of Mother Teresa and on the other, we are disheartened as we read in the papers accounts of destructiveness and cruelty around the world. We need concentrated inner attention to keep in focus what really makes us human: compassion, loving concern for the other. This awareness helps us become increasingly more sensitive to the inter-connectedness of all people.

This workshop is designed to help us identify with the "other," especially the poor, the homeless and strangers. By working with the sayings of Jesus in Matthew 25:31-46 ("I was hungry and you gave me food"), we search for our connectedness with others. By this process, we may become ready to relate to other humans in the wider world in new ways. Such shifting is

For additional reading on the development of these themes, see Joanna Macy, *Despair and Personal Power in the Nuclear Age*, New Society Publishers, 1983.

accomplished by sensing our feelings, listening to our bodies and engaging our imagination. Emotions of anger or even hopelessness over conditions around us may be evoked. This stage is part of a process that can lead us to express our care for the world. We deepen our realization that our own well-being is woven into and dependent upon the well-being of all.

Imagine a room filled with dancers. Everyone is connected, lightly touching one another with a hand, foot, hip. The dancers are instructed to be sensitive to the slightest change in movement and to react to that change. One dancer is instructed to fall forward. All feel the pull, those closest are affected the most, but the configuration is now changed.

The directions are then reversed. Everyone is still connected as before but now are told to *resist* responding to the stimulus. As a person falls, great effort is required to maintain balance and equilibrium. (The leader may choose to enact these exercises at the end of the introduction.)

"Playing" through dance enables us to perceive things in fresh ways and to reduce the fears that underlie our resistance to change. Ezekiel was speaking about this capacity to change when he said: "And I will give them one heart, and put a new spirit within them; I will take the stony heart out of their flesh and give them a heart of flesh, that they may walk in my statutes and keep my ordinances and obey them. They shall be my people, and I will be their God."

Ezekiel 11:19-20.

Yet, I have heard people ask, uneasily, "What good will it do to feel compassion when I can't do anything practical to help?" or "I have too many problems of my own!" or "The problem is too big for one person to handle." We begin by making small changes within ourselves. Part of the numbing feeling of despair over large issues come from the fact that we don't allow ourselves to express and act upon our own personal life situations.

Invocation

Preparation: Place a candle in a central position. Ask all to sit cross-legged or in a comfortable, but prayerful, position.

We come together in meditation. We focus our minds and hearts, and pray, stilling our inner and outer selves, opening ourselves to receive grace and the insight needed for spiritual growth. Slowly breathe . . . in and out . . . Feel connected to the candle. Bring the light into your heart, the center of your being. (The leader may reach out to the candle and then bring her hands toward her body, as if drawing the fire to herself. Some may naturally follow and imitate this gesture.) Fire gives warmth and energy. Fire also purifies, transforms. Feel the warmth and light enter into every part of your being. Reach with your hands toward the fire . . . a gesture from the dawn of time. (Pause) Please close your eyes and sit with your palms opened, facing upward. Let the words from Matthew enter into your heart:

I was hungry and you gave me food,
I was thirsty and you gave me drink,
I was a stranger and you welcomed me,
I was naked and you clothed me,
I was sick and you visited me,
I was in prison and you came to me.

Matthew 25:35-36.

Ubi Caritas

The leader demonstrates the following movements and all repeat, while chanting or following the music:

Taizé Chant

Ubi caritas et amor

Place hands in front of the heart. With a gentle flowing motion, stretch arms forward and sideways, palms turned outward, with a blessing.

Ubi caritas, Deus ibi est

Curve arms in front of the body, as if gathering a child or sheltering someone, and bring toward your heart. Repeat, imagining people you wish to gather to you with love.

The leader prays:

Spirit of the universe, forgive us for any harm we have done to ourselves, to other living creatures, and to our environment. May we be guided to become more aware of the needs of others.

May peace be in my mind, on my lips, and in my heart.

Bring your hands together, palm to palm; focus your energy and slowly touch your forehead, lips, and heart. Cross your arms over your chest and fold into a reverent bow from the waist. Hold for a moment and gradually unfold. Moving from the heart, slowly reach out your arms as if to touch all people; visualize linking your heart to all living beings. Greet your neighbors.

Theme Work

The following exercises are intended to help us feel, see, and be empathetic with different kinds of persons in need, and to face our underlying resistance to being "in touch with others." The first set of exercises deal with harmony and the second set with lack of harmony.

Breath Flow

We begin by creating movement in harmony with the rhythm of our breath. Our breath is like a living stream of water, endlessly bountiful. The leader asks the group to sit as in meditation, comfortably, with the spine erect, each focusing attention on his/her body and breath.

Leader: Breathe in deeply, picturing a stream of water flowing into you. Breathe out, like a fountain giving forth its waters. Slowly repeat, three or four times, allowing the breath to fill and empty from a deeper and deeper place. With eyes closed, add a simple arm movement to each breath. Feel your arms and torso moving together, organically, from the heart. Allow the flow of movement to find a natural completion before it is drawn back into the next breath. Continue for a few minutes.

Shapes of Harmony

We begin with shaping harmonious movement, aware of the dance elements of weight, flow, energy, and time that makes movement life-giving. What are some "shapes" of caring? For example, when we see a mother nestling her child we may notice the curvature of her arms, the rounding of her body, the harmonious design of both their bodies, the strength in her arms and back as she carries the child. The leader now demonstrates movements that are rounded, circular, and curved, with the group following. After a couple of minutes the leader asks the group to improvise their own circular movements, making sure to include the breath flow. Each person begins by moving alone; gradually the participants are drawn into relationship by moving around each other in space and connecting their circular patterns. The leader encourages them to change levels, rhythm, and dynamics. Designating small groups, the leader asks them to experiment with ways to bear the weight of one another, supporting each other. The improvisation ends with all being drawn into one harmonious shape.

Movement without Breath

The leader demonstrates simple movements, such as arm extensions, that have no breath connection, with the chest hardly engaged. It feels rigid and lifeless. It is important for the group to see the difference between movement that comes from the heart, with breath, and movement that is directed by the brain, but bypasses the heart. After observing this demonstration, the participants try simple patterns of their own, paying attention to the feelings induced by movement that lacks breath and connection.

Shapes of Disharmony

What are some designs of the body that reflect disdain, anger, hardness of heart? Ask two people in the group to demonstrate with a tableau a typical scene of alienation, such as conflict in a family, tension in the street, isolation between individuals.

The leader now demonstrates movements that are straight and angular, rather than curved and rounded, and gradually distorts them more and more, with the group following, as in the previous exercise. After a few minutes the leader stops, and the group continues in its own way. The leader directs the participants to move with increased intensity, including contracted, inwardly directed movements. Focusing on their own feelings of anger or frustration or hatred they quickly find shapes to express them. The leader reminds them to draw upon the isolation exercises, from the previous session, as an aid to finding movement. After a few minutes of exploring these shapes by themselves, the participants work in small groups, experimenting with conflicting and inharmonious shapes.

Building a Bridge

The leader requests each person to make two body shapes. The first, using the conflicting movement shapes, reflects a feeling of despair, anger or hopelessness about the suffering in the world. The second, using harmonious shapes reflects feelings of joy, love, or hope if these sufferings were alleviated.

Each person is to move from the first shape to the second shape, observing the transition in the movement. The journey is like crossing a bridge, moving from despair to hope, from isolation to connectedness. Take some time to shape the two positions carefully. Gradually let the body assume the first shape, hold it for a few seconds and then gradually move toward the second shape. Hold the second shape. Reflect on the feeling of "crossing the bridge."

Group Study: The Beggar

This study is to be done quickly, with a sense of urgency and excitement. It rapidly warms people up to the theme. Designate one person to play the role of the beggar—as on a typical city street—facing at right angles to the crowd of people passing by the block. His hand is outstretched.

Direct the others to line up, one by one, and to file past the "beggar," walking, running, expressing different reactions through their body movements.

Note: I have seen many varied reactions—people turning their heads away, going behind the beggar, quickening their pace, secretly putting something in his hand. One person had a most illuminating action: he walked toward the beggar with his head held high. As soon as he passed him by, his body crumpled. It was as if something *in him* had died. At a recent workshop, it was suggested we walk like the homeless.

Opening the Heart

Reading the Scriptural Text

We will apply what we learned from the previous work to the Gospel of Matthew. Read Matthew 25:31-45 aloud; then pause. The passage is like a beam of light, directing us to the neglected and discredited person, calling us to open our eyes and see, open our hearts and feel, open our ears and hear, and desist from turning our backs. We are called to respond to the needs of the least of the people—the poor, the sick, those in prison, and to act with compassion.

I believe Jesus is giving us a very important clue as to who *we are* by his words, "If you did not do it to the least of these, you did not do it to me." He is saying that he identifies with "the least," that he is not separate from them and neither are we. If to know and see Jesus we must be able to see him in others, then to know ourselves we must be able to see ourselves in others. It is startling to speak to another person and to realize that person is representing in his or her body an aspect of yourself! We are being led into a mystery. We are separate and unique souls, but we are not separate. My good is your good; your good is my good.

Beginning the Study

Ask all to stand, each in his/her own space as if each person was in the privacy of his/her own room. They are to respond with body positions as you call out slowly the following words extracted from the passage: "I was *hungry* . . . (I was) *thirsty* . . . *a stranger* . . . *naked* . . . *sick* . . . *in prison.*" The response should be quick and spontaneous, an immediate reaction to the word rather than one that is thought out and designed. It need not literally depict the word. For example, to the word "naked" the response might be a position of "shame."

All take partners. One person will be called A, the other, B. Ask the A's to find a body position and hold it while you read, "I was hungry . . . " Ask the B's to respond to their partner's position as you continue ". . . and you gave me food." Pause. Everyone is now in pairs, each couple having formed a unique "living sculpture" of the above phrase. Ask all to move in reverse order. As you read "I was thirsty," the B's take a shape, and the A's respond at the words ". . . and you gave me drink." Continue in this manner.

Variation: Ask half the people to assume positions of need, but with *no words spoken aloud*. Their partners are called to respond only to what they see and feel.

The Jeopardized

Matthew 25:42-45

We now turn our attention to the second part of the passage. It is a warning, a call to awareness. Through movement we can become more conscious of our feelings, and realize the effort and "armaments" needed not to be compassionate!

The leader reads Matthew 25:42-43:

> *. . . for I was hungry and you gave me no food, I was thirsty and you gave me no drink, I was a stranger and you did not welcome me, naked and you did not clothe me, sick and in prison and you did not visit me . . . "*

All participate in a discussion of why people avoid helping others. Discuss types of people in need that you avoid, and what you can't stand about them. What are their circumstances and environments? What attitudes underlie lack of concern with one's neighbor? Examples that have been given include arrogance, self-righteousness, indifference, self-absorbtion, fear, one's own pain, frivolity, following the crowd, disgust.

Preparation for the Dance

Each A chooses one of the categories of need to work with, such as being "hungry," or "sick," or "in prison." The categories chosen need to be relevant to the A's own inner life, i.e., the A's must first reflect on their own poverty, hunger (for what?), thirst, imprisonment. They thus dance drawing on the feelings of their own deprivations, physical or psychological, as well as trying to incorporate the public aspects of street people, or others in varying depressing circumstances. The leader may wish to ask participants to compose an alternate litany to bring home the encompassing nature of Matthew 25. For example, "I was homeless, and you took me in. I had AIDS, and you took care of me. I was lonely and you held my hand. I was angry, and you listened to me . . ."

When the music begins, each A will concentrate only on his/her role, exploring in depth the movements and feelings contained in that state. The A's each choose one place in the room to work in, keeping relatively close to that place as they dance. It may be at the periphery of the room, such as along one of the walls or in a corner; or it may be more centrally located. They move primarily with torso, arms, and head. (This will not be a problem, since they are in "prison," "sick," "alone on a street bench," etc. Curtailing movement in space will help intensify the movement from within.)

Each "B" chooses one negative attitude and corresponding lack of response and finds a typical movement pattern to express it. As with the A's, the attitude should be close to home, not just theoretical. It will take a few moments to discern what the attitude and movement is for each B. For example, a movement of self-absorption might be to literally wrap one's arm around oneself while walking ("wrapped up in one-self"), or an ambivalent movement that leads to avoidance, such as changing direction when you see a beggar.

The B's move around the room and will pass by the A's without taking any notice, or with suitable reactions according to each one's character. This will continue for an uncomfortable amount of time. It takes awhile before the surface movements subside and the repressed less "pleasant" feelings and movements emerge. The point is to become more aware of these feelings as the dance goes on. Both A's and B's take several minutes to explore their characters and movements.

The leader calls the group together to begin the study. The B's take places at the periphery of the room while the A's go as they please. When the music begins, the A's move, entering into their character. After about two minutes the B's begin their movement patterns. The B's are free to move about in space, improvising in groups or alone. The music becomes softer after five or six minutes. The A's drift slowly to the right side of the room. The B's drift to the left side of the room. After both groups are at their respective sides, the leader moves to the center with outstretched arms, reaching toward each group—as if to bridge a great chasm—as if stretched on the cross.

As the music stops all freeze.

The leader draws the group together to discuss what took place. The following are suggested points for discussion:

- How did you feel when the B's passed you by and failed to help?

- How did you feel when you had to keep ignoring the A's?

- Share examples from your own life of this kind of tension.

- How do you feel now after expressing this tension through dance?

At the insurance office
I got extremely interested
in the insuring of hands.

What value should be put on
the hands of artists?
the hands of doctors and nurses?
the hands of athletes?
the hands of writers?

What, or what value should be put
on hands that beg for alms, or give,
on hands that pray,
on hands that raise You, Lord?

Dom Helder Camara, *A Thousand Reasons for Living*, Darton, Logman and Todd, London, 1981.

The Opened Heart

In the final stage of our study, we dance to proclaim the vision of Matthew 25:35-46. The leader asks all to join with their partners of the beginning study. Dancer A is the subject of the dance. The leader allows a few minutes for the dancers to choose their part. The dancers do not reverse roles for each part is complete in itself.

Dancer A chooses a scriptural image from the text for the study, e.g., moving from hunger to fullness. Dancer B will dance with A, sometimes side by side, sometimes mirroring the movement, sometimes following dancer A; and sometimes leading dancer A. B's task is to unite inwardly with A and express this outwardly, being part of A's healing process. At the conclusion of the dance, each set of partners bless each other, laying hands on one another's heads.

Rite

The closing rite consists of two dances, *O Lord, Hear My Prayer*, and/or *Sound over All Waters*.

O Lord Hear My Prayer

Stand and form two concentric circles facing center. The leader demonstrates the dance and suggests that while the dance is being performed, participants call out prayers loudly above the music. This works best at the first part of the chant when all are facing center.

O Lord hear my prayer

Begin with the left hand in front of the chest, palm turned upward. In a continuous motion, pass the right hand across the upturned palm of the left hand and lift it upward, in front, as if calling to God.

O Lord hear my prayer

Return the right hand to the left, placing both over the heart. Bow slightly forward.

When I call

Lifting the torso, stretch both arms upward, palms facing forward.

Answer me

With arms still reaching upward, sway first to the right and then to the left. As you are swaying to the left, continue the motion of both arms to the left side and downward, ending in front of the body. This movement flows into the next.

O Lord hear my prayer

O Lord hear my prayer

All face right, or counter-clockwise, and take 4 steps (2 for each refrain) beginning with the right foot. The torso is bent slightly forward and the arms are stretched out in front. Palms face upward and fingertips point ahead to the ground, as if blessing the way. On each step the torso gradually rises and both hands slowly lift upward.

Come and listen to me

Bring the feet together while still facing right. With hands upturned, circle the left arm overhead and bring it to rest, palm facing downward, on the upturned palm of the person behind you in the circle. On "to me" all bend knees in unison, pulsing down and up. Turn and face center to begin again.

Note: Repeat the pattern as many times as desired. Remember, it takes awhile for a new movement prayer to take hold, for each person to enter into its rhythm and patterns as if they composed it themselves.

Sound over All Waters

This closing dance meditation is designed to uplift and unite. The song recalls the angel's proclamation of peace on earth, of glory to God and good will to all. Dancing joy and hope releases and expands our feeling of connectedness. We feel ourselves to be part of a larger whole. Sr. Mary Beth Reissen, S.N.D., Pax Christi's representative to the United Nations, remarked, "The dance makes me aware of the power of goodness. Through the dance we know we are connected. It takes more than words."

All are invited to stand, close together, with eyes closed. Sense with your body all the people around you, and allow the music to enter your soul.

> Sound over all waters reach out from all lands,
> The chorus of voices, the clasping of hands;
> Sing hymns that were sung by the stars of the morn,
> Sing songs of the angels when Jesus was born
> With glad Jubilation bring hope to the nations.

Feel as if water is moving around you and through you. Respond with small, sideways movements of your spine as if you were plants swaying in the tides of an estuary. At the words "clasping of hands," all reach out to the side with their right hands, and then with their left hands, until all hands are clasped. These movements are done with feeling and accent, catching the impulse of the song. All sway together, hands joined, moving as one. Sink down together, bending your knees. Slowly all hands lift upward, still swaying, with the upward movement timed to reach its peak by the first note of the chorus.

That dark night is ending,

On "dark", hands release and shoot upward. On "night," all bend forward, arms swinging down and behind the body. On "is," come to an upright position, cupping hands in front of the torso, at about heart level. On "ending," extend arms outward and sideways with an accent, as if opening shutters.

And dawn has begun

Repeat the phrase.

Rise, hope of the ages,

Inspired by Arthur Hall, a dancer/actor who conducted an experimental session with the Omega Dance Company to this musical setting.

On "rise, hope," swing and cross arms in front of the body and open them outward to the sides. On "of the ages," lower your arms with a circular motion, cross them in front of you, lift them over your head and open them, like the spreading rays of the sun.

Arise, like the Sun!

Repeat the second movement pattern.

All speech flows to music, all hearts beat as one!

Repeat the first movement pattern twice, as before.

The dark night is ending

Repeat the second movement pattern

And dawn has begun!

Draw hands toward your heart, curving your torso inward, open your arms outward, like the sun's rays, turning in place.

Music Interlude

All move in a milling around fashion, extending first the right hand to one person and then the left hand to another as you greet each and move on. Halfway through the music the leader slows the group down, and all gradually come to a pause. Hands join, linking in all directions, as you lean, sway, and dip to the floor, trusting and supporting one another. (This can form a beautiful interconnected and organic, maze-like structure).

Repeat Chorus.

Second verse

The leader, taking someone's right hand with her left hand, begins a snake dance, or "peace line," that moves around the space. The leader makes sure that all are back together in the center before the final chorus.

Repeat chorus as before. End by stretching arms out in all directions, sending forth blessings of peace.

>>>>>

WORKSHOP MATERIALS

Listed below are the materials and music for Workshop II. The leader may wish to substitute music according to availability. Care should be taken to match the feeling and tone of the suggestions. The leader may also choose to work in silence, and/or with live accompaniment.

Invocation
Materials:	Candle
Music:	Meditative
	See suggestions in Workshop I
	Ubi Caritas from *Taizé in Rome*, 1981
	GIA Publications Inc.

Warm-Up   See Workshop I.

Theme Work

Breath Flow and Shapes of Harmony
Materials:	None
Music:	Harmonious
	The Road Less Taken from *Pianosong*, Paul Halley, Living Music
	Moonbathing from *Susan*, Susan Osborn, Living Music

Movement without Breath and Shapes of Disharmony
Feeling:	Discordant, arhythmical
	live drumming
	electronic selections
	George Crumb (various recordings)

Building a Bridge
Feeling:	Soul music, gospel, jazz
	Trouble of the World from *Bless This House*, Mahalia Jackson
	Jean Luc Ponty recordings
	A Simple "Kyrie" or "Agnus Dei"
	Gregorian or Modern Chant

The Beggar
Feeling:	Disquieting
	Live drumming

The Study

The Jeopardized
Feeling:	Inner directed, searching, groaning
	Hearing Solar Winds from *Current Circulation*, Harmonic Choir, Celestial Harmonies
	The Opened Heart
Feeling:	Searching, uplifted
	Alleluia, from *Harmonic Meetings*, David Hykes & the Harmonic Choir, Celestial Harmonies
	Ponty, Jean Luc recordings

Rite
Music:	*O Lord Hear My Prayer* from *Wait for t the Lord*, Taizé, GIA Publications, Inc.
	Sound Over All Waters, from *Signature*, Susan Osborn, Lifeline Recordings, PO Box 848, Eastsound, WA 98245

WORKSHOP III

Dancing on Holy Ground

"They shall not hurt or destroy
in all my holy mountain;
for the earth shall be full of the
knowledge of the Lord
as the waters cover the sea."

Isaiah 11:9

Introduction to the Theme

The photograph of the beautiful blue and white earth, suspended in space, has slowly and indelibly changed our perception of the world. The image, like leaven in bread, is rising in our consciousness. It is an icon of peace.

The American astronaut Rusty Schweikert, while on a space flight, saw "that the oceans of the world bordered nations without regard to political beliefs." He saw "one planet, with one people . . . and he came to the startling sensation that the planet was alive, that it was Mother Earth . . . and that she was weeping."

Quoted by Norman Runnion in the Bennington Banner, 8/17/89.

The concept of peace on earth is indivisible. It encompasses the whole of creation. In this workshop we seek to strengthen our connections with the natural world and dance as partners with the whole of creation. We lift up the covenant of peace made by God with Noah and every living creature.

"Behold, I establish my covenant with you and your descendants after you, and with every living creature that is with you, the birds, the cattle, and every beast of the earth with you . . ."

Genesis 9:9-10.

Thus the Scriptures remind us that God's covenant includes three primary parties: God, humanity, and nature. Looking at the state the world is in today might lead one to deduce that

See "Uniting Friends with Nature", Marshall Massey, reprinted in *Network News*, the International Network for

45

Religion and Animals, Vol. 1, No. 6, Winter, 1988.

the covenant was two-way, between God and humankind with nature merely to serve our needs.

The covenant has been ruptured. We seek to open our hearts and live harmoniously with nature, thus attending the creatures as Noah did, under God. This workshop aims to invoke in each participant a willingness to re-establish the broken, segmented covenant. This covenant is a key to the continuity of our life and the life of our planet. We begin by transforming our consciousness through dance as we strive to become allies and advocates for the natural world: providing sanctuary to animals, insuring clean air and water free of pollution, and safeguarding mountains and forests from wanton destruction based on economic motives of gain.

We find in both Isaiah 24:4-6 and Leviticus 26:3-4 the connectedness of justice and the conditions of the earth. The earth reflects back to us either our caring attitudes, or our economic, exploitative values and actions. If we mistreat the earth, there will be suffering. God will not save us from the consequences of our actions.

We begin with an attitude of reverence and humility before the mysterious life of the earth, each particle of which is imbued with the presence of God. In Exodus 3:2-6 it is recounted that Moses was startled to see a bush burning in the wilderness. He approached it to see why it was on fire but was not consumed. Then the Lord spoke from the bush and told Moses to take off his shoes, for he was standing of "holy ground." We "take off our shoes" to stand connected to the holy crossroads of life.

St. Francis is a model and leader for us. His heart was "full of the knowledge of the Lord." He was a troubadour and dancer on the holy mountain. He had a knowledge of the ways of the creatures, knowing how to speak to the birds and how to tame the wolf. Sleeping in the open air, with a rock for his pillow, he listened to the soft footsteps of many creatures, and became intimate with their ways.

At the end of his life, as he lay dying in his cell, blind and suffering, he composed his paean to life, the famous *Canticle of the Sun*. In the canticle he pours forth praises of the natural elements, the earth, air, water, and fire, addressing them as brother Sun, sister Moon, brother Fire, sister Water . . . singing of their beauty and calling them close, dear companions of his body and soul. He was allied to nature.

The first part of our study is called *Becoming Allies*. We begin by dancing the unique beauty and gifts of creatures. Through dance improvisation, we expand our ability to identify with other life forms. With this increased closeness, we may find ways to help shape the forces that can lead to their protection and fulfillment. Like St. Francis we bend our knees and listen to their speech.

The "creation" saints and mystics are re-emerging into the foreground as we seek to counter the image of the natural world being destroyed, of native people vanishing, of the earth ending in nuclear waste.

St. Francis was a peacemaker. One story tells of his making peace between the town of Gubbio, Italy, and a fierce wolf who was terrorizing the villagers. I think he could do so, because he knew how to tame his own "inner" wolf. He was not only concerned for the villagers though. Before he left, he taught them how to care for the wolf's needs. St. Francis modeled himself on Jesus, who "did not count equality with God a thing to be grasped, but emptied himself, taking the form of a servant." Now is the time to empty ourselves of our human arrogance and become protectors of the rights of all creatures.

Philippians 2:6-7.

We are standing at a crossroads where a conscious choice can be made, between healing and preserving our habitat, or joining in the mindless destruction of the environment.

The second half of our study is called *Becoming Advocates for Creation*. We prepare the way for the holy ground; where no one is hurt nor destroyed. Our model is St. Patrick, the fiery saint of Ireland. Like St. Francis, he is known for his strong connection with the natural world. Once he called on the elemental forces to come to his assistance and stand between him and "the forces of darkness." He invoked "the sun, with its brightness, and the moon, with its whiteness, and the fire with all its strength.

This invocation is part of what is known as St. Patrick's Rune.

St. Patrick was troubled and tormented, on fire for God's kingdom. His fervor can be a model for us. We, too, are troubled and tormented, with the protective ozone layer of the atmosphere being destroyed, and rain forests and species of animals and wildlife disappearing.

Dancing our prayers and hopes is a unique form of social action. We will dance with consciousness and power, blessing the earth, sanctifying it as a dwelling place for all—for the birds, fish, animals, rocks, people, sky, sea.

Dancing on Holy Ground

Invocation

Place a candle in a central place in the room, visible for all to see. Ask participants to sit in a prayerful, attentive position, focusing on the light.

Leader: Slowly breathe, in and out, connecting yourself to the flame, bringing the light into your heart, the center of your being. (Pause) Flame purifies, transforms, gives warmth and energy. Feel the warmth and light enter into your body. With St. Francis we say, "My Lord be praised by Brother Fire."

Leader demonstrates the following movements, and all repeat the words and movement together:

Come Holy Spirit, fill the hearts of your faithful and enkindle in us the fire of your love . . .

Arms stretch sideways, palms upturned. With an upward motion hands cup overhead, in the shape of a flame. The flame is drawn downward, ending in the heart.

Send forth your spirit and we shall be created and you shall renew the face of the earth.
The cupped hands turn outward, and moving from the heart they stretch forward, in an outward expanding motion, sending out a blessing.

Leader: Please stand, face upturned, eyes closed. Your arms are by your sides, with palms facing forward. Breathe in deeply. As the chant begins (*Veni sancte spiritus* - Come Holy Spirit) slowly raise your arms upward, palms facing toward your body. Then lower your arms, hands passing only a few inches from your face, and moving down your torso, like a blessing of rain, or of mercy, falling from the heavens. Bend slightly forward and bring your hands toward the center of your body. Slowly straighten and reach with your hands outward, as in the preceding prayer. It is as if the Holy Spirit is emerging from within you.

Repeat the movement pattern for *Come Holy Spirit* (see above) as many times as you like, with your own timing, allowing it to become your prayer for the creatures. Over the chanting of *Veni, Sancte Spiritus*, the leader calls out names from the list of endangered animals. The entire list from the Interior Department numbers over 950. The following is a sample listing of endangered and threatened species.

Mammals: Antelope, armadillo, ass, baboon, bandicoot, bat, bear, beaver, bison, bobcat, camel, caribou, leopard, tiger, cheetah, chimpanzee, chinchilla, cougar, deer, eland, elephant (African, Asian), ferret, fox, gazelle, gorilla, hare, ibex, jaguar, kangaroo, leopard, lion, lynx, manatee, marmot, monkey, mouse, ocelot, otter, panda, panther, possum, prairie dog, rat, rhinoceros, seal, sloth, stag, tapir, tiger, vicuna, wallaby, whale, wolf, wombat, yak, zebra.

Birds: Albatross, booby, broadbill, condor, crane, creeper, cuckoo, curlew, eagle, falcon, finch, flycatcher, hawk, kestrel, macaw, ostrich, parakeet, parrot, pheasant, shearwater, stork, thrush, vireo, warbler, woodpecker, wren.

Reptiles: Alligator, boa, crocodile, iguana, tortoise, turtle, viper.

Amphibians: Coqui, frog, salamander, toad.

Fishes: Catfish, chub, dace, darter, gambusia, madtom, pupfish, sturgeon, sucker, trout, woundfin.

Snails: Snail (nine varieties).

Clams: Pearly mussel, pigtoe, stirrup shell.

Crustaceans: Amphipod, crayfish, isopod, shrimp, Kentucky cave.

Insects: Beetle, butterfly, moth, naucorid.

Meister Eckhart counsels that the artist should interpret the verse 'The Holy Spirit shall come upon thee' (Lk 1:35) to mean: 'The Holy Spirit shall come from within thee.' *Meditations with Meister Eckhart*, Matthew Fox, Bear & Co., Santa Fe, NM, 1983.

For more information, write to Endangered & Threatened Wildlife and Plants, U.S. Dept. of the Interior, U.S. Fish & Wildlife Service, Washington, DC.

Theme Work

Ruby-throated hummingbird: *"During courtship the female sits quietly on a perch while the male displays in a pendulum dance, swinging in a wide arc and buzzing loudly with each dip."*

(Audubon Society Field Guide to North American Birds, Eastern Region)

Our interconnectedness with creation can be made more personally vivid as we reconnect with our personal "creatureliness." Dance is one way to explore and become more aware of our creatureliness as we creep, crawl, jump and leap, moving joints and limbs in endless, natural ways. From earliest times people have danced the movements of animals, wind, lightning, and other natural forces surrounding them. By imitating and learning the habits of creatures, people were helped to hunt them or acquire their power. Today, we dance to experience on a feeling level our kinship with all creatures. In intuitive, bodily ways we may connect with their adaptiveness and responses to life, their spirit and special beauty. Thus we may be motivated to learn of their needs and help in their protection.

The leader places pictures and other material on endangered species at one side of the room. Then all are asked to walk from picture to picture, studying the material in silence. After a few minutes, the leader invites all to move around the room exploring the different movement qualities of the animals. Then everyone gathers at one side of the room to cross back and forth according to these suggestions:

- gentleness - move as gently as a doe, in the forest, at dusk.

- swiftness - move as quickly as a hawk, streaking through the sky - as a pelican diving into the ocean.

- fierceness - move with the strength of the tiger on the prowl, gathering momentum for the leap.

- playfulness - move as a dolphin thrusting itself over and under the waves.

- follow additional suggestions from the participants.

Everyone lies down on the floor as if they were St. Francis sleeping in the open, with a rock for a pillow. We are dreaming with St. Francis. He cries out in his sleep for he is a troubadour who can't sing any more because the birds are being silenced. He cries out again for his spirit cannot soar or take wing, because the wings of birds are covered with oil and they are drowning. He cannot roam the woods, because his friends, the coyotes and wolves, are being hunted and their territory narrowed.

This study was inspired by work pioneered by Joanna Macy and others in what is known as "deep ecology." They have devised a ritual called *The Council of All Beings*, wherein humans listen to the creatures of the earth speak of their needs for survival and of their unique and irreplaceable gifts to the planet. It is a moving vision of mutuality and respect. See Seed, Macy, Fleming and Neass, *Thinking like a Mountain*, New Society Publishers, Philadelphia, PA, 1988.

He no longer hears the little underground creatures because the foxes with their great long ears are being hunted and extinguished. He wakes up with a fright and dances—dances the gifts of each of the creatures who are a part of him.

Allow yourself to be drawn by your spirit to one creature that has a special attraction for you. You will create a brief dance/movement study from your meditation. The study will include some aspect of the creature's unique beauty and spirit, and may also include something about how that creature needs our help. For example, in Northern Ireland, as a response to this study, one older woman came crawling into the room on her stomach, as a mother seal. She lifted up her white head, made "seal" sounds, and then said, "I am beautiful, and innocent. I need help. They are slaughtering my children." Another man, who was actually lame, hobbled forward with dignity and pathos, and offered, "I am a rabbit. They have caught my feet in a trap!"

When the participants have returned and are ready to share their studies, the leader divides them into groups of three. Each person shares the study with the group, both verbally and in movement. The group learns some of each person's study. (In the second half of the workshop this same group becomes a support team for one another as needed.)

When everyone has shared, the participants come together. The leader plays music and invites all to dance their creatures simultaneously.

Becoming an Advocate

Study

This study was inspired by an account of St. Patrick. In the story St. Patrick keeps demanding blessings from an angel, implying that he has a right to make his demands because he "has been tormented." He threatens that he will not leave from the rick, or mountain, 'til he has been blessed with his wishes. In the end, it is the angel who gives in, and all St. Patrick's demands are granted.

We will emulate the saint and be fierce and demanding, practicing being bold in our defense of the creatures and the rest of creation. We recall the boldness of St. Patrick's Rune, wherein he even asks the sun, the moon, wind, rocks and water to come to his assistance.

The leader asks all to spend a few minutes in silence and choose one issue involving justice for the life forms of the planet that he/she feel strongly about . . . sets him/her on fire!" Each person silently formulates his/her concern into one phrase or sentence. For example, "that rain forests be destroyed no more!"

When all are ready, the leader asks them to form two concentric circles. Sticks, or woodblocks, are distributed to the outside circle. A mark is made in the center of the inside circle.

Bamford and Marsh, "St. Patrick on Cruachan Aigle," *Celtic Christianity, Ecology and Holiness*, Lindisfarne Press, MA, 1982, pages 54-58.

The form of the dance is explained and practiced, and people volunteer to be "advocates," or "adversaries."

The outer circle, beating their sticks, slides (or chasses) clockwise. The inner circle slides counter-clockwise, with hands joined. The pace is fast. All chant:

Burning Bush, Holy Flame
Holy Spirit is Your Name!

Repeating the chant, both circles converge toward the center and back out again. Both patterns continue, alternating back and forth. The circles are like rings of fire.

After three patterns of the chant, the first *advocate* makes her way through the rings of fire and stands on the center spot. She shouts with passion her concern (for example, "that the cutting down of the rain forests be ended!") and adds, "I have been tormented, I will not leave, 'til I am blessed!" The circles stop moving and take up her chant, changing the sentence into a prayer. For example, "May the rain forests of the world be saved . . . May the rain forests of the world be saved . . ." They crouch or kneel, as they chant, so that the center action can be seen.

An *adversary* steps into the center, yelling "Get thee gone!" and challenges the strength of will of the *advocate*. This takes the form of a danced "tug-of-war," in which the adversary tries to pull the advocate from her spot. If the advocate gets weak, she can call on her team for help or the strength of creation itself. After a few minutes of the combat the adversary concedes, releases her grip, pauses and blesses the advocate. As she blesses the advocate she blesses her request, saying, "Let us bless the rain forests of the world." Everyone repeats the blessing, lifting hands, chanting, "We bless the rain forests of the world." Both advocate and adversary join the circles, another advocate and an adversary take their places to begin the ritual anew. Note: If time permits, the group discusses the "adversaries" of today and how they threaten the life of the planet.

Rite

Concluding Prayer Dance

We have danced to bless the animals and other life forms of the earth, aligning ourselves with their future well-being. But it is difficult to rejoice and celebrate when we hear of species vanishing and the earth being defiled. Our concluding dance will commemorate and mourn the passing of creatures from the face of the earth, expressing with our whole beings our hope for the renewal of the planet.

The leader asks all to form concentric circles.

Leader: As you stand, consciously feel the connection of your feet, gently, yet firmly, to the floor. Feel the balls of your feet, your toes, your heels, and even the muscles in your feet. We can bless with our feet, and be blessed. The blessing takes place

Adapted from *Woman Prayer/Woman Song* by Miriam Therese Winter, Medical Mission Sisters, PA, 1987, p. 49.

I acknowledge with gratitude the following groups who have participated in the formation of this rite: Temenos, Sacred Dance Guild Festival, Pacific School of Religion summer dance students, Chinook Community, and Kirkridge Retreat Center.

Workshop III

through our connectedness to the ground, even if it is covered with stone and cement. What matters is your awareness of this connection of foot to surface. Slowly rock back and forth, and feel this connection.

The Blue Green Hills of Earth

This beautiful, majestic song is found in the **Missa Gaia**, or Earth Mass of the Paul Winter Consort. There are three verses, a musical interlude, and two concluding verses. The movement pattern is the same for all the verses. The circles move in opposite directions, clockwise and counter-clockwise.

> *For the earth forever turning;*
> *For the skies, for every sea;*
> *To our Lord, we sing returning*
> *Home to our blue green hills of earth.*

All join hands and take three slow steps forward and one step backward, beginning with the right foot. This pattern is repeated three times. On the fourth musical phrase, all release hands and circle around themselves in place, arms lifted, blessing. (Repeat sequence for each verse.)

Note: Imagine with each step that you are ascending the "holy mountain", accompanied in an invisible way by the creatures.

Musical Interlude

The leader calls out the names of creatures that have been danced in the studies, adding names from the list of endangered species. Participants converge to the center and kneel and touch the floor, with bodies bowed. Then they rise and move into a shape of one of the creatures for whom they wish to pray. It will look like a living sculpture of many animals. At the end of the music they resume their places in the circles.

Final Verse

The movement sequence is the same until the end when all face center and stand in prayer with hands joined, arms lifted.

>>>>>

WORKSHOP MATERIALS

Listed below are the materials and music for Workshop III. The leader may substitute music according to availability. Care should be taken to match the feeling and tone of the suggestions. The leader may also work in silence, and/or with live accompaniment.

Invocation

Materials:	Candle, List of Endangered Species
Music:	Meditative

Songs of the Indian Flute, John Rainor, Jr. Red Willow Songs, Box 51, San Carlos AZ 85550; or other Native American recordings.

Veni Sancte Spiritus from *Cantate!*, Taize, 1981 GIA Publications, Inc.

Warm-Up   See Workshop (1).

Theme Work

Music: Environmental music, varied, suggestive of wildlife

Drumming for the Shamanic Journey, Dolphin Tapes, PO Box 71, Big Sur, CA, 93920.

Drumming, Steve Reich, Nonesuch.

Live drumming or flute

Hand Dance, Frame Drum Music, Music of the World, P.O. Box 258 Brooklyn, NY 11209.

African Funeral Song from *Nexus*, Paul Horn, Epic

Study

Materials: Pictures and material on endangered animals and environmental concerns; sticks or woodblocks; marker for central spot

Becoming An Ally

Music: sparse, evocative

Songs of the Indian Flute, Red Willow Songs, Box 51, San Carlos AZ 85550.

Becoming an Advocate

Music: Exciting, driving, rhythmic

Drumming, Steve Reich.

Journey of the Drums (A), Musart Inc. PO Box 20968, Oakland CA 94619.

Rite

Materials:	List of Endangered Species
Music:	**The Blue Green Hills of Earth** from

Missa Gaia/Earth Mass, Paul Winter, Living Music

WORKSHOP IV

The Way of the Beatitudes

Introduction to the Theme

I have been pursuing the beatitudes, like koans in Zen, for nearly twenty years. While the method of pursuit may be felt by some to be unusual, I try to understand the beatitudes by choreographing them into dance movement.

The beatitudes touch upon the deepest human feelings and concerns. These realities are in some way part of our individual or communal experience; they are deep within our body memory. Through meditation and exploration, our bodies can express their richness. Jesus *saw* the people, let them know that he felt their needs, and cared. They were no longer invisible. The objective of this workshop is to bring forth the beauty, simplicity and challenge of the beatitudes through the physicality of dance.

Dance and prayer are the means we choose to connect to the physical and spiritual power of the beatitudes. This workshop assists us to become more conscious of our feelings, and to experience the blessings of the journey.

I remember a liturgical dance by Robert Yohn. Two dancers kneel and touch the floor with reverence, as the narrator says, "Blessed are . . ." The dancers then rise and touch the floor in a different place as the text continues.

The Man They Say, choregraphed by Robert Yohn.

As the dance was being performed, I was struck both by the sparseness of the dancer's movements and the power of what was left unsaid. The dance gave me open space to complete each beatitude in my own heart. I felt a wordless prayer as though uttered and grounded each time the dancers touched the floor. The movements recalled to me lines from Isaiah: "How beautiful upon the mountains are the feet of one who brings good news, who

Isaiah 52:7

heralds peace, brings happiness . . ." Momentarily, I envisioned the dancers following a path, and the path was the way of the beatitudes.

For me, the beatitudes evoke the beauty of hidden realities which lie deep within the recesses of the heart. Outwardly, the beatitudes seem so contradictory. Who would want to be persecuted in order to be blessed? But considering the reality of life and each person's struggles, we see through the contradiction and recognize their worth. In the historical setting, they were addressed to people who experienced poverty and persecution, and I believe, like rain on parched soil, are understood in time of need as a source of blessing.

Murray Bodo writes: We speak of the Gospel, and he (an American Indian) says, "It is like Blessingway. There is no Gospel, no Blessingway without social justice." I am stunned by the use of a formal term like "social justice," and he sees my surprise. "If you are in need and I hold my corn bundle and pray for you, but give you nothing to fill your need, there is no blessing for you or for me. There is no Blessingway if I am selfish with my material goods."

Murray Bodo, *Meditations from the Desert.*

This phrase was the theme of a Summerfest at the Corrymeela Community, Northern Ireland.

The beatitudes have been perceived as describing an "upside down kingdom," a time of transformation, when our own world has been turned both inside out and upside down. Through the fluid medium of dance we can experience an authentic flow of movement, which in turn can become a transforming movement of the spirit in our lives.

Henri Nouwen writes: "On August 6, 1945, while Christians celebrated the Transfiguration of Jesus on Mount Tabor, the nuclear era was inaugurated by a light that incinerated Hiroshima and killed 75,000 of its inhabitants. On that day the blessing on peacemakers became the blessing for our century."

Henri Nouwen, *A Spirituality of Peacemaking*, Part I, New Oxford Review, p. 8.

Invocation

Preparation: Place a candle in a central position. Ask all to sit cross-legged or in a comfortable, but prayerful position.

We come together in meditation. We focus our minds and hearts, and pray, stilling our inner and outer selves, opening ourselves to receive grace and the insight needed for spiritual growth. Slowly breathe . . . in and out . . . Feel connected to the candle. (Pause) Bring the light into your heart, and the center of your being. (The leader may reach out to the candle and then bring her hands toward her body, as if drawing the fire in. Some may naturally follow and imitate this gesture.) Fire gives warmth and energy. Fire also purifies, transforms. Feel the warmth and light enter into every part of your being. Reach with your hands toward the fire . . . a gesture from the dawn of time.

Let the hands return to rest at sides or lap. Close your eyes and listen to the beatitudes. Let the words sink into your consciousness. Let the spoken words have power. When Jesus said to a sick man that he was healed, he was healed! Let us listen to the beatitudes as if Jesus is speaking to us now.

We are being blessed as we listen. Our bodies, our whole being, are absorbing the sound of the words, enabling them to become part of our danced prayer on an unconscious, intuitive level. Be at rest, let your heart listen.

The Beatitudes

> *Blessed are the poor in spirit, for theirs is the kingdom of heaven.*
> *Blessed are those who mourn, for they shall be comforted.*
> *Blessed are the meek, for they shall inherit the earth.*
> *Blessed are those who hunger and thirst for righteous ness, for they shall be satisfied.*
> *Blessed are the merciful, for they shall obtain mercy.*
> *Blessed are the pure in heart, for they shall see God.*
> *Blessed are the peacemakers, for they shall be called the children of God.*
> *Blessed are they that are persecuted for righteousness sake, for theirs is the kingdom of heaven.*
> *Blessed are you when some shall revile you and persecute you, and shall say all manner of evil against you falsely, for my sake.*
> *Rejoice and be exceedingly glad; for great is your reward in heaven.*

Matthew 5:1-12

Blessed are the poor in spirit. Bend forward and make two fists. Hold them tightly, in front of you. (Pause) Relax your hands very slowly, and at the same time uncurl your back. Open your hands with palms turned upward. How, or what, do you feel? (Pause)

The poor in spirit are those who recognize their need for God, and in humility open their hands and hearts . . .

Leader: Spirit of the universe, forgive us for any harm we have done to ourselves, to other living creatures and to our environment. May we learn new ways to be in harmony with the life of our planet. May we be guided by the way of the beatitudes.

May peace be in my mind, on my lips, and in my heart.

The prayer concludes with a gesture. Bring your hands together, palm to palm. Focus your energy and slowly touch your forehead, lips, and heart. Cross your arms over your chest and fold into a reverent bow from your waist. Hold for a moment and gradually unfold. Moving from the heart, slowly reach out your arms as if to touch all people, visually linking your heart to all living beings. Greet your neighbors.

Workshop IV

Theme Work

Meditation

The meditation flows from the Invocation. The leader begins by reflecting on the meaning of the beatitudes in a free-form way. This is to prime the pump. The participants will be asked later to contribute their own insights, verbally and in dance.

Blessed are the poor in spirit: those who know they need God—whose hands are open, empty—beggars for the spirit—non-materialistic—open to the unconscious—to the kingdom of heaven—poverty of spirit is the first of the beatitudes—the rest flow from it. Yet each beatitude is also its own doorway, opening to the kingdom of heaven.

Based on God's covenant of Genesis, we are all created in God's image, and every person has a right to the basic resources of life. We should not romanticize the poor, implicitly sanctioning the condition of poverty. The "kingdom of heaven" belongs to those who empty themselves to help alleviate the suffering of the poor. The young man of the Gospel is asked to sell his possessions and give his money to the poor. Voluntary poverty (involving a radical reorienting of one's life style, as practiced by the Catholic Worker people, for example) is not to glorify poverty, but to stand side by side with those who are in need, witnessing to God's compassion.

Matthew 25:31-46

Blessed are those who mourn: those who have lost a mother, a father, a lover, a friend—those who are not cut off from their feelings—those who care about others, and feel their suffering.

The key to the beatitude of mourning involves opening ourselves to pain in and around us, and offering consolation. Comforting is a gift of community. In Isaiah, comforting those who mourn is a sign of the spirit of God anointing us. There are those who mourn because of natural causes, and those all over the world because of injustice, brokenness of spirit, despair, or feeling trapped in poverty. We may find ourselves mourning the destruction of the earth, the wanton death of countless creatures and life forms.

Blessed are the meek: those who practice gentleness, humility, non-violence—those who care for the earth and the conservation of life—those who are teachable, open to new experiences.

This beatitude seems so contradictory. Generally, the meek have no possession of the land, but only care for it while others profit. In our consumer society we exploit the land, and one wonders what will be left to inherit. Jewish spirituality involves the coming together of God, the people and the land in a holy relationship. This is exemplified by the injunction to rest from work one day a week, and to allow the land to lie fallow one year, every fifty years—the year of Jubilee. When we live with a sense of God's presence in the world, all is a gift from God, for the benefit of all. We can no longer hold so tight a grasp on our right to absolute ownership, as if what is given for the common good can be destroyed for private profit.

Blessed are those who hunger and thirst for righteousness: those who are aware of the rights of others and who care passionately for justice—who devote their lives to better the conditions of others.

Reflecting on this beatitude after the disturbances in Los Angeles which followed the Rodney King case, I viewed the chaotic destruction, looting and burning in part as a desperate cry from people hungering for vengeance and thirsting for justice. The distribution of wealth, as well as protection from racism and classism, are certainly basic issues of justice. We realize many person's "needs" often represent luxuries when other people's basic minimal rights are not met. The desperate people who looted the stores in Los Angeles will not be satisfied by television or other consumer goods, but such material possessions have become distorted symbols of the right to possess what others have. Justice is a constitutive part of God's covenant with all creatures. Chaos in the community reflects our blindness to the demands of justice.

Blessed are the merciful: those with the gift of forgiveness, mercy, compassion—who are moved by the plight of others—who acknowledge our humanness—you draw to yourself the qualities you give.

This beatitude flows directly from our concept of covenant: God's covenant with us, and through that our covenant with one another. Time and again we break our covenant with each other, but each time we are to forgive one another—as many as "seventy times seven." God forgives and is just, and we are made in God's image, called to be just and merciful in turn. When we are not, the flow of the covenant is broken. If we wish to reflect God's perfection, we are called to be merciful on an individual, group and institutional level.

Blessed are the pure in heart: those who see with clarity both inwardly and outwardly—living in forgiveness brings purity—singleminded—seeing God in the beggar, the streetpeople, the homeless.

How the beatitudes interweave! Purity of heart represents total commitment to God's plan. Inner dedication to God's ways is manifested by sharing with those in need. Seeing God in the poor, in the homeless, in the stranger is part of living the covenant. Thich Nhat Hahn, a Vietnamese monk who was well aware of the horrors of war, practices what he calls "Engaged Buddhism." He invites us to learn to focus and be aware, so that we may really see others and thus be enabled to become truly compassionate. When artists strive to purify and clarify their concepts, they witness purity of heart.

Blessed are the peacemakers: those who day by day listen, see and desire the good of all sides—those whose own being radiates peace and understanding, enabling them to reconcile

Matthew 25:37

Thich Nhat Hahn, *A Guide to Walking Meditation*, Nyack, New York: Fellowship of Reconciliation, 1985.

divisions—those who work for peace—who allow violence to stop with them.

Peace is based on justice. The peacemaker is called to be aware by searching for the seeds of war within, as well as on an outer, worldly level, for otherwise destructive powers are set in motion that develop their own life. For example, when corporations protect their interests by their owners equating them with the country's good, these need to be dealt with in a corporate way. At a Berkeley teach-in following the Rodney King verdict, an African American director of urban studies expressed his deep concern over the future of justice in the United States. He concluded his speech quoting Isaiah, "Whom shall I send . . . (and he looked around) . . . Here am I. Send me!"

Blessed are those who are persecuted for justice' sake: those who act with integrity and take the consequences—through suffering one can become Christlike, a deep channel of overflowing, transcendent love. The last beatitude is the summation of all the preceding ones.

The early church was a persecuted subgroup. Those who may be persecuted today are not always called the "church," or "Christian," but they may be those with whom Jesus threw in his lot, the outcast, and alienated. Jesus both lived and put the beatitudes into practice. I pray that we and "the church" will have the grace and courage to do likewise. If we do, we will experience the beatitude blessings. We will be living within the covenant, rejoicing in the task of contributing to a new creation.

(Pause)

The leader asks each participant to choose a beatitude which has special significance for them. As the leader repeats the litany, each rises when their selection is called, and spontaneously creates a gesture, or full-body position expressing the feeling the beatitude invokes. Each person's gesture gives expression to a unique response from the heart.

The leader instructs them to fix this position in their minds, so that they can later visualize the shape, and feel the effort or energy embodied in the position.

Working with the core gesture

The leader selects one person with a striking body position and demonstrates how the gesture can become the seed or kernel of an extended phrase of movement. For example, the leader, while maintaining the recognizable shape of the gesture might change levels (up or down), move in space, vary the rhythm and intensity of the movement. The point is to release the energy of the gesture in different ways.

The leader asks all to form their core movement/gesture, and to feel it intensely. They are given two or three minutes to experiment in movement with their core gesture, finding release and direction for the energy contained within it.

The leader then asks one or more volunteers to teach a phrase of movement based on the core gesture to four or five individuals in the group. As each group demonstrates their movement in unison, the rest observe the power of the expanded gesture.

Dance Meditation

The following dance meditation employs the full use of the body. One movement should flow into the next with the leader determining the timing.

Blessed are the poor: moving through space, slowly open your hands, feeling vulnerable, empty, ready to receive. Closing and opening your hands, extend the movement to the rest of your body by opening your torso and then contracting. Breathe deeply, in and out.

Blessed are those who mourn: wrap your arms around yourself and rock back and forth. Reach toward someone, lean on and support one another.

Blessed are the meek: still supporting one another, bend over and slowly move across the floor, as if you were a refugee carrying your remaining possessions on your back.

Blessed are those who hunger and thirst for righteousness: reach with your arms upward, letting them rise and fall. Clasp hands with others and together release from within a cry for peace and justice.

Blessed are the merciful: move slowly, leading with your heart. Feel heavy. Shape your arms as if you were gathering to yourself the weight of the world. Rock with a feel of accepting the burden of care. Turn to a person next to you and link fingers. Rock back and forth in the same direction, as if you were cradling something precious between you.

Blessed are the pure in heart: move slowly, in a sustained way, as if drawn to something by an inner awareness, as if you hear a beautiful melody, as if drawn to a precious flower.

Blessed are the peacemakers: walk slowly toward someone who is at a distance from you. Pretend this is someone who has a grievance against you . . . after an interval, slowly extend your hand.

Blessed are the persecuted: clasp your hands behind your back, as if tied together at the wrists. Move backward as if pulled and drawn against your will, your body reacting, twisting turning. Pause. Release your hands and let your body slowly collapse.

Rejoice and be exceedingly glad: slowly begin to move, as if you are in a beautiful garden with a wonderful breeze, sunlight pouring over you, the fragrance of flowers filling your being, renewing every cell.

Study

The leader divides the participants into groups according to the beatitude they originally chose. The groups separate to reflect and share, both verbally and in movement, what the beatitude means to them. They will then create a study based on the beatitude. The study may develop from the core movement gestures or be expressed in a new way. The group may work in unison, or structure an improvisation that enables people to participate in individual ways. In addition to the non-verbal dance, each group writes a few lines that express their insights about the beatitude.

Note: The very process of working together in a group is an exercise in peace-making. It is natural for leaders to emerge, and for people to think differently. If a member feels strongly that he/she is moving in a different direction, either he should work in a corollary way to the group or leave and work alone or with another group.

Rite

Preparation: A table is arranged with nine vigil candles, plus a taper. The center candle is lit. Branches or flowers may be placed around the candles to heighten the beauty of the table. A bell or gong is at the side. A jar of water, bowl and branches are placed below the table. A basket of rhythm instruments are within reach. The participants gather in a semi-circle before the table, leaving enough space for dancing. The leader instructs them on the form of the ritual and teaches the shalom chant described below.

Dancing the Beatitudes

The ritual begins with the leader, standing by the side of the table, striking the bell. A member of the first group comes forward, lights a candle with the taper, lifts it high and in a clear voice recites the beatitude. The rest of the group comes to the center and takes the opening position of their study. The written reflection is shared and the dance study performed. (The studies may vary in length, usually from two to five minutes.)

At the conclusion of each study the following chant is sung and danced by everyone except the group who has performed. They remain in their final dance position to experience the chant as a blessing.

Sing shalom

Arms lift with a forward and upward movement, palms facing out, blessing. Head and torso follow the upward movement of the arms.

Sing shalom

Arms lower, torso bending slightly forward.

Sing shalom, peace on earth

Hands rise with palms placed together, wrists turn so that the back of the left hand faces outward. Fingertips point upward. Wrists rotate so that the back of the right hand now faces out outward, and descends on "peace on earth."

Sing Shalom

Hands separate slightly, then cross and circle overhead, fanning outward, and return to the traditional prayer position.

The above ritual order is repeated for each beatitude. The leader initiates the sequence each time by striking the bell.

Celebration

It was a custom in the early church and during the Renaissance to dance what was known as the "ring-dance of the angels." The angels were believed to have danced with the "blessed." In the following dance we can imagine that we are joined by the angels. There are two versions to choose from; version one is more simple.

Rejoice, rejoice and be exceedingly glad, for great is your reward in heaven. (twice)

The leader ceremoniously pours water from the pitcher into a bowl. The bowl is held waist high by another participant. The leader puts the pitcher down, picks up the branches, and dips them into the bowl.

In thy kingdom, remember us . . .

The leader dances slowly and ceremoniously, sprinkling the group lightly with water from the branches. The person carrying the bowl accompanies the dancer among the group.

Version 1

> *Blessed are the poor in spirit . . .*
> the chant continues through . . .
> persecuted for righteousness sake,
> *for theirs is the kingdom of heaven.*
> The bowl and branches are set down and the leader indicates for all to join hands and follow her. She leads them into a spiral, or snake dance to the center of the room, and unwinds the group, retracing her steps to form a circle.
> Blessed are you when some shall revile . . .
> *against you falsely, falsely, for my sake.*
> All stop, facing center, and bow their heads.
> *Rejoice, rejoice and be exceedingly glad,*
> the chant continues through
> *. . . great is your reward in heaven.*

This is a variation of the sign language for peace.

This dance is set to *The Beatitudes* composed by Jim Scott, the music of which is part of the *Missa Gaia (Earth Mass)* of the Paul Winter Consort, commissioned by the Cathedral of St. John the Divine, New York City, to celebrate the feast of St. Francis.

Workshop IV

The leader, while continuing to dance, brings forward the basket of rhythm instruments and places them in the center of the circle. Participants choose instruments and everyone dances in a free-form manner, improvising to the rhythms of the music.

Version 2

> *Blessed are the poor in spirit . . .*
> the chant continues through
> persecuted for righteousness sake,
> *for theirs is the kingdom of heaven.*

Movements contributed by Stephen Coleman, member of the Omega Dance Co.

This is done in a spiral or concentric circles with the following basic pattern. With hands joined, facing center, all step sideways to the right with the right foot, then forward and toward the center with the left foot, backward with the right foot and to the right by crossing the left foot in back of the right foot. This four-step pattern is repeated until *Blessed are the poor* is repeated in the music and a new variation is added: step sideways to the right with the right foot and touch the left foot to the right; step forward with the left foot and touch the right foot to the left; step backward with the right foot and touch the left foot to the right foot, and cross the left foot behind the right foot and touch the right foot to the left foot. This pattern can be augmented by adding free body movement and touching with a bounce or skip.

> Blessed are you when some shall revile . . .
> *against you falsely, falsely, for my sake.*
> All stop, facing center, and bow their heads.
> *Rejoice, rejoice and be exceedingly glad,*
> the chant continues through
> . . . great is your reward in heaven.

The four-step pattern with the "touch" step continues, with the following arm gestures: step to the side with the right foot and open arms sideways, shoulder height, palms facing forward. Step to the center with the left foot and swing both arms forward with palms facing front. Step backward on the right foot and swing arms backward. Step with the left foot crossing in back of the right and swing both arms to the left in a welcoming gesture to the person on your left.

As the tempo increases, *great, great, is your reward . . .*, begin a new step, moving in double time: step sideways to the right and touch left, step sideways to the left and touch right, step sideways to the right and cross the left foot in front of the right foot, step sideways to the right and touch the left to the right. Reverse directions.

Repeat the above a few times and then add the last step: With both legs together bounce to the right, to the left, and double to the right (the second bounce with a dip). Reverse to the left. Have fun!

WORKSHOP MATERIALS

Listed below are the materials and music for Workshop IV. The leader may wish to substitute music according to availability. Care should be taken to match the feeling and tone of the suggestions. The leader may also choose to work in silence, and/or with live accompaniment.

Invocation

Materials:	Candle
Music:	Meditative
	Silence for the opening
	Amazing Grace from *Datura*, Susan Osborn.

Theme Work

Music:	Feeling: Expansive, evocative
	The Road Less Taken from *Pianosong*, Paul Halley.
	Full Circle from *New Friend*, Friesen, Halley
	African Funeral Song from *Nexus*, Paul Horn, Epic

Study

Materials:	Paper and pencils
Music:	Silence

Rite

Materials:	Table, nine vigil lights, taper, branches and flowers, bell, jar of water and bowl, a basket filled with rhythm and other instruments
Music:	Participants from each group decide if they want to be accompanied with previous meditative music, bells, drum, or silence

Shalom, traditional Jewish melody

Beatitudes from *Missa Gaia*, Paul Winter Consort

The Peace Rite

Our closing rite centers around the ancient custom known as "agape." Agape, a Greek word for love, was the name used for the common evening meal of the early Christian church. The gathering was characterized by warmth and joy and an openness to all, especially the poor, and was set in the framework of psalms and prayers. Our celebration will include bread and wine, traditional Judeo/Christian symbols of gifts from the earth.

Our rite of celebration incorporates materials from the previous workshops as well as new elements. The structure is as follows:

> Entrance Dance
> Call to Worship
> Reading
> Response in words and movement
> Peace Litany
> The Bringing of the Gifts
> The Blessing of the Gifts
> The Sharing
> The Closing

Preparation. A central table is set with candles, flowers, and Scripture. A table in the back is set with cups of wine and a basket of bread. The leader has a basket with seeds. Rhythm instruments are placed conveniently. Everyone gathers at the entrance of the room with the leader facing the group. Green branches or stalks of flowers are distributed and placed in front of each person. They will be incorporated in the opening and closing dance, which is taught beforehand.

I'm going to lay down my sword and shield
Down by the riverside

Other elements may be added according to the discretion of the leader and the cultural make-up of the participants. At an Interfaith Service designed by Allan Tung for the Sacred Dance Guild Meeting, 1987, mead (a drink from ancient Greece); milk (for Hindus); beer (for Africans); and water (for Buddhists) were incorporated as ceremonial drinks common to a variety of cultures.

71

This music can be found on the tape, Mahalia Jackson, *Bless This House*, PCT 8761.

The opening movement suggests casting your burdens and defenses to the ground. All stand, facing the leader, hands held in fists in front of the body. As the song begins, everyone slowly lunges forward, simultaneously opening their hands and extending their arms forward and downward toward the floor.

Down by the riverside, down by the riverside

All rise and repeat the previous movement.

I'm going to lay down my sword and shield
Down by the riverside

All rise and once again repeat the casting down movement.

Ain't goin' to study war no more.

All pick up their branches and raise them overhead.

Chorus: Ain't goin' to study war no more. (6 times)
All dance into the room or down the aisles holding their branches high, and waving them from side to side. This is repeated after each verse.

Each of the verses are danced in the following manner:

The pattern is in the form of a "grand right and left" as the dancers move informally from person to person, rather than maintaining the traditional circle formation. Everyone places both branches in their left hand and extends their right hand in a clasped greeting. They alternate, passing the branches from one hand to the other, the free hand extended for the greeting. This is repeated throughout the verse, with people passing in all directions, moving from one to the next. At the conclusion, the branches are placed on the floor, around the table.

Call to Worship

O Sacred Spirit, O Divine Breath of Life, open our ears that we may ever hear your continuous canticle of creation. Open our hearts that we may sing in harmony the goodness of creation. Release our spirit that we may dance your praise and glory. Amen.

Reading: Matthew 13:31-32

The kingdom of heaven is like a grain of mustard which a man took and sowed in his field; it is the smallest of all seeds, but when it has grown it is the greatest of shrubs and becomes a tree, so that the birds of the air come and make nests in its branches.

Response to the Reading

The response is divided into two sections: discussion and dance. Jim Wallis, editor of *Sojourner* magazine, writes: "There is only one way of being able to see a large tree of justice when you are looking at a small seed in the palm of your hand." He noted it required the "eyes of faith (that) don't despise small beginnings".

Jim Wallis, "Seeds of Faith", *Sojourner*, May, 1985.

Discussion. What have we done together during these past sessions that has changed you? What has allowed you to plant new seeds of hope? What "small beginnings" can you take in your own life? How can we water our seeds and care for our plantings?

Dance of the Seeds

Part I: Planting the Seed

Preparation. The leader reminds them that the grain of mustard seed can be likened to a small gesture, that contains much potential . . . a telephone call, a letter to a friend or congressman, a handshake, a cup of water.

The participants are asked to consider the "grain of mustard seed" in their lives, and to choose one word that is needed to bring about the kingdom of God (for example, *love*, or *imagination*, etc.). The leader then asks: And what do we need for the kingdom of God? One person rises, as if holding a "seed" that will flower, and proclaims a key word for the kingdom, such as *love*, or *faith*, or *hope*, or *imagination*, etc.

Leader: And what will bring in the kingdom of God?
Another rises with "seed" and responds with another word.

The litany continues in the above fashion until all are standing. The leader teaches the dance.

All stand close together with the left hand placed heart level, with the palm cupped upward. The right arm is stretched straight overhead, forefinger and thumb touching, as if holding the seed.

As the music begins, in slow motion, lower your right hand to your left palm. When it makes contact, fold your body over and lower yourself to the floor, curling into a small shape— a mustard seed of faith. Close your eyes. At your own timing, allow your seed to crack and break open. This may take the form of tentative movements of your head, chest, hands, or legs. Explore, reach out, as if absorbing the nutrients from the earth, as a seed takes in air and water and minerals as it mingles with the soil.

After a minute reach toward one another and feel a connection. Slowly open your eyes and allow yourself to be affected by the movements of those around you. Move as one organic life form, coming together and rising like a tree with a common root, bursting into life with shoots, leaves, branches, flowers and fruit. Pause as the music concludes. The leader moves through to the center, holding the basket of seeds. The group remains in place for the next section.

Part II: Scattering the Seed

Leader: We dance like we are the wind, with driving force and energy. As the wind scatters the seeds upon the earth,

The Peace Rite

so we scatter the seeds of our faith. Let us dance with thanksgiving and praise!

Begin moving slowly, with your body bent forward, arms swaying in front of you, palms face downward, as if you are dispersing the seed upon the face of the earth. Move around in all directions, changing levels, and gradually pick up tempo. Your feet pound on the floor, as if beating the seeds into the soil, while your hands are blessing the ground. The leader dances ceremoniously among the group, with the basket of seeds. The following prayer may be read over the drumming accompaniment.

> Seeds.
> Whole, to be broken,
> dry, moist,
> searching for a home, a nesting place, fruition.
> Veni, veni, sancte spiritus,
> breathe hope,
> breathe healing,
> breathe laughter, forgiveness, safety, peace...
> breathe a new spirit into me.
> Winds of beauty, winds unwinding, nourishing the soil,
> opening the shells,
>   sending down the roots, lifting up the tendrils,.
> *May we live!*

Everybody is dancing simultaneously, with freedom and abandonment.

Introduction to the Peace Litany

Leader: Let us gather together and open our hearts in prayer to the spirit of Love.

May the spirit lead us to reveal our needs
and to identify with the needs of others. (all sit)

Peace Litany

All raise hands and intone the words for peace in any language, e.g., peace, shalom, salaam, mir . . .

The following words may be included in the peace response: peace, *paz* (Spanish), *pace* (Italian), *paix* (French), *frieden* (German), *mir* (Russian), *salaam* (Arabic), *shalom* (Hebrew), *ho ping* (Chinese), *heiwa* (Japanese), *shanti* (Hindi Sanskrit), *wolankoto* (Dakota Sioux), *shlomo* (Syriac), *oboto* (Zairean), *amani* (Swahili), *malu hia* (Hawaiian), *eirene* (Greek), *suhl* (Swedish, Danish, Norwegian), *Khaghagut'iun* (Armenian) . . .

1. For those who are poor in spirit,
   that God's kingdom be theirs.
   PEACE RESPONSE
2. For those who are sorrowful,
   that they shall be consoled.
   PEACE RESPONSE
3. For those who hunger and thirst for righteousness' sake,
   that they may have their fill.
   PEACE RESPONSE
4. For those who make peace,
   that they shall be called daughters and sons of God.
   PEACE RESPONSE
5. For those who show mercy,
   that they may receive mercy.

PEACE RESPONSE
6. For those who are persecuted for holiness sake,
   that the kingdom of God be theirs.
   PEACE RESPONSE
7. Let us voice our own needs and concerns.
   (Pause for silent and voiced prayers)
   PEACE RESPONSE

Leader: Loving God, we present our prayers to you, mindful of how deeply we are interconnected. May peace flow like water in the desert as we offer each other the sign of peace.

The Passing of Peace.

The Bringing of the Gifts

Introduction. We now focus on the table and the elements of bread and wine for the sharing as we sing from "Word of Truth and Life" from *The Mass of Creation* by Marty Haugen.

Beginning with the first verse, two participants slowly process forward toward the center table, carrying the bread and wine. They pause on the "Alleluia" while the group follows the gestures of the leader. By the last verse the gift bearers are behind the table, holding the gifts high for all to see.

Alleluia

All lift arms upward, with wrists circling inward and outward (as if spinning a rattle) with a flowing quality.

Alleluia

Keeping arms lifted, arms cross overhead and open outward and upward, with a flowing quality.

Praise the Word of Truth and Life

Arms swing downward and back upward, with a clap on the upswing. Arms slowly lower, palms facing downward, toward the table, blessing the bread and wind.

Blessing of the Gifts

Leader: Loving God, Giver of All Good Gifts, we are grateful for all that you give us.
All: We are grateful for all that you give us.

Leader: You feed us and nourish us with friendship and care.
All: We are grateful for all that you give us.

Leader: God of all Creation, we are mindful that sun, soil, and gentle rain has blessed this bread and wine. We are grateful for all that you give us.
All: We are grateful for all that you give us.

Leader: Bless us as we eat this bread and drink this wine in a holy manner.
All: Amen.

The Peace Rite

The Sharing

The bread is now broken and placed in the basket and distributed.

The Closing

Leader: Blessed are you, loving and creating God. Blessed are you,

All: Blessed are you.

Leader: You never sleep, but keep a watchful eye over all you created. Blessed are you.

All: Blessed are you.

Leader: Blessed are you, guardian of peacemakers. Blessed are you.

All: Blessed are you.

Leader: May the peace of God be in our minds, on our lips, and in our hearts. Amen.

All: Amen

Dance Celebration

Participants pick up the branches and instruments, such as drums, rattles, etc. The process around the room and outside, as the following lines from Isaiah are read or chanted:

> "For your shall go out in joy,
>   and be led forth in peace;
> the mountains and the hills before you
>   shall break forth into singing
>   and all the trees of the field shall
>   clap their hands.
> Instead of the thorn shall come up the cypress;
>   instead of the brier shall come up the myrtle;
> and it shall be to the Lord for a memorial,
>   for an everlasting sign which shall not be
>   *cut off."*

Isaiah. 55:12-13

Any concluding dance may also be used. We suggest **Sound Over All Waters**.

WORKSHOP MATERIALS

Listed below are the materials and music for the Peace Rite. The
leader may wish to substitute music according to availability.
Care should be taken to match the feeling and tone of the suggestions. The leader may also choose to work in silence, and/or with
live accompaniment.

Entrance Dance
Materials:	Green Branches or Flowers
Music:	**Down By the Riverside**, *Bless this House*, Mahalia Jackson, PCT 8761

Call to Worship
Materials:	None
Music:	None

Reading and Response
Materials:	Basket, Strip of paper, pencil *Planting the Seed*
Materials:	Basket with seeds
Music:	*Cantate!* Taize (see above) (Pater Noster)

Scattering the Seed
Materials:	Basket with seeds
Music:	**Pondero** from *Hand Dance*, Glen Velez *Journey of the Drums* (Side A) 1

Peace Litany
Materials:	Text
Music:	None

The Bringing of the Gifts
Materials:	Table, cups of wine, basket of bread
Music:	**Word of Truth and Light** from *Mass of Creation*, Marty Haugen, GIA Publications

The Blessing and Sharing of the Gifts
Materials:	Same as above
Music:	None

The Closing
Materials:	Drums, rattles, branches
Music:	**Sound Over all Waters** from *Signature*, Susan Osborne, P.O. Box 848 Eastsound, WA 98245

The Peace Rite

Epilogue

For indigenous people there is no separation between sacred and secular dance. Dance is integral with the on-going life of the community. Artistic and entertainment values are subsumed into the overall purpose, and dances are rich and satisfying for body and soul. Dance has beauty and function. Like prayer, it can be hard work, but ecstatic. Dance is a resource for life. Imagine fine art and folk forms of dance and prayer combined and grounded in vital functioning for the community.

Between 1976 and the present, as an artist-in-residence at the Cathedral of St. John the Divine, New York City, I had opportunities to choreograph and share in the creation of many communal experiences for events of far-reaching significance. I wish to note one political, one interfaith, and one ecological example, all representative of our efforts to integrate the arts with peacemaking.

The Soviet-American Celebration in February, 1988, brought about a communal experience of the congregation together with several hundred Russian and American leaders and scientists dancing in the great crossing of the cathedral. They circled around a weather balloon representing the world, while surrounded by children with candles. Dance, music, prayer, and speech coalesced to give expression to our hopes and dreams. For the Spiritual Summit Conference VI, in 1985, Allan Tung, associate choreographer with the Omega Company, created a living "mandela" of dancers as a symbol of interfaith understanding.

For ten years, the annual *Earth Mass*, for the Feast of St. Francis, with the Paul Winter Consort, has been a prototype and celebration of our aim to co-exist respectfully with God's entire creation. With changing patterns and dynamics the dancers mirror through their bodies the grandeur and scope of the liturgy: they solemnly process, bearing incense; they race down the aisles proclaiming life for the creatures, as we hear wolf calls mingling with Paul Winter's saxophone; they leap and bound in harmony to the rhythms of whale and ocean. Finally, as the *Canticle to Brother Sun* is sung, the whole congregation joins with flowing gestures. This event, which draws more than five thousand people, unites in music, dance, and prayer creatures ranging from microscopic organisms to elephants, in an astounding paean of praise.

Martha Graham noted that dance is a practice for the art of living. I believe dance can be both a practice and a prayer, teaching us to connect head and heart with our actions. What you dance you cannot easily forget, for it becomes assimilated into your very being. Dance is both a metaphor and a way of peace, reuniting us, body and soul, with the greater whole. I maintain that dance, like liturgy, is the work of the people. When well-done, the celebration is rich and inspiring. Simone Weil writes, "Let the soul of (man) take the whole universe for its body." It is a difficult but inspiring task. May we be privileged one day to celebrate with the universe, rejoicing in a truly great dance!

We offer these workshops and rites to the end that dance, with its non-verbal, unifying gifts of integration, may become a real resource toward understanding "the ways that make for peace."